MW00647153

A SYNCHRONOUS MEMOIR
OF ADDICTION & RECOVERY

Aaron B. Bryant

JUNE 2010

A SYNCHRONOUS MEMOIR
OF ADDICTION & RECOVERY

Aaron B. Bryant
Edited by Michael Riquino

ISBN: 978-0-615-37922-7

Printed and made in USA

Cover & Book Design by Brant Skousen

I have been awake for five days now.

I am walking the streets of Salt Lake City. Purposefully. Gotta get some money. My thoughts are scattered, loose, erratic, but I know I must find a way to get some money. I am walking down North Temple Street when I see the sun peeking over the horizon. To my right, a transient man pushing his grocery cart. To my left, in the plasma center parking lot, a man slumped over and hanging out of a car. Is he dead? A closer look...it appears he has been shot. The lady in the wheelchair. Does she see him? No, she's just waiting for the center to open to give her plasma donation. How ironic. There's enough blood on the ground to save several lives. The car looks out of place, like it was pulled to a quick halt, like it doesn't belong there. His feet are still in the seat, but his upper body is hanging out of the car. It's laughable, surreal. It's tangible and grizzly. I look at the only 25-cent payphone left in Salt Lake City that I know of and think for a second that I should call, but I don't want to deal with that— with the police report. I am in a hurry. I have to catch a train across town if I'm to get this money. Gotta get some money.

Gotta get h i g h . . .

I began playing the piano at the age of four. As one of the youngest pianists my instructor had ever taught, I couldn't even reach the foot pedals initially. I played soccer, I played the piano, I was learning to read. I was gifted and mature.

One of my first piano recitals conflicted with a soccer game, so my performance was placed at the end of the program with the advanced students to accommodate. I arrived at the recital in full uniform: shin guards, soccer cleats, and grass stains on my knees. I marched down the aisle amidst snickering from the audience and sat down at the piano. The piece was advanced for my age group, but I played it with ease, without hesitation, making no mistakes, and leaving the room shocked at my premature talent. I stood up in front of the large audience and walked confidently out of the auditorium like a self-proclaimed rock star, head held high and soccer cleats clicking on the tile.

My mother educated me in reading and mathematics at a sixth grade level prior to starting kindergarten. My academic skill set was years ahead of my age and this early start helped me excel in school. I made the honor roll every year. By the third grade I had begun taking private art lessons and was becoming increasingly creative, especially when compared with my similarly aged classmates. I was invited to attend Beyond the Basics, a summer program for advanced students. This program allowed me to take computer classes long before other students even had computers available to them. My interest in learning continued to grow. I can recall working on an Apple computer with a group of classmates creating an intricate and complex presentation on the nature of the galaxy. Our presentation included slideshows, video clips, and research information that would be the envy of many high school students.

My childhood was truly ideal. Family life was suburban, almost cliché. There was no dysfunction in my family, immediate or extended, no divorces, no mental illness, no criminal problems, no substance abuse. These were good, happy, successful, traditional families. My father worked while my mother stayed at home. He was the breadwinner and she was the soccer mom. The neighborhood I grew up in was full of the same: functional families where children played football with their fathers on the weekend. Anything less was completely foreign.

The stability and family bonding present in my early childhood revolved around our active involvement and mutual interest in sports. We had opportunities that simply weren't available to other families. We attended many sporting events as a family and often had season tickets to the Salt Lake Golden Eagles, a NHL hockey farm team, and to the Utah Jazz, our favorite NBA basketball team. We sat in the fourth row for the Utah Jazz next to two wild ladies who dressed in the team's attire, painted their faces, and spent the game on their feet yelling at the referees. These ladies knew all of the refs by name and would often badger them for any call made against the Jazz. This provided a great source of laughter for my family.

My father attended all of my games and even coached my recreational soccer team one year. We spent nearly every weekend together playing soccer, baseball, and football. During Sunday night football games, I would run around the living room with a football pretending to be Barry Sanders, my favorite football player, and pestering my dad during half-time to go outside and play catch with me. He always obliged and I always tried to impress him with my new moves. This never failed to bring a smile to his face. It was moments like these that I felt truly alive, truly loved. The love of my family fostered my ambitions and I believed I could do or become anything.

FATHER

We were like twins. My father meant everything to me. He was my soccer coach for a year, he always attended my bowling league competitions, he was never too busy to play ball in the backyard, he was the biggest influence on my childhood self. We even had the same intellectual interests: world wars, space and the universe, lost civilizations, and we both loved to eat out. There was no one I looked up to more. My father meant everything to me.

My father decided it was time to replace the roof on our house, so he hired friends from around the neighborhood to help. My father was a handyman and rarely hired anyone to fix anything he couldn't fix himself. He was also the main manager at an Acura car dealership, so he hired some of his men there to help as well. Because I was only in fifth grade, I was told I could not be on the roof. I was assigned to pick up the pieces that had been stripped from the roof.

I hated this. I was furious. I wanted to be part of the guys, I wanted to be on the roof helping, and mostly I wanted to be working alongside my father. I ran inside and into my room, sulking on my bed. I even began crying while I sat on my bed feeling sorry for myself. This is when I heard my mother say, "Is he all right?" I immediately got up and ran outside. Everyone was confused. One of the lot men from my father's work wanted to do CPR. My father had collapsed and was lying down in the bed of a truck. I had learned CPR in Boy Scouts. I was so confused. I talked my father's employee through the process. Compressions. Breaths. It felt like I was dreaming, everything moving slowly, my body shaking, compressions, breaths, everyone was confused...

The ambulance finally arrived and I had to watch my father be shocked in an attempt to get his heart beating again. This was too much for me, too much for a child my age. I broke down. Tears streamed down my face and I couldn't stop trembling as my father's body jerked with each shock. My father was taken away and I didn't even know if he was still alive.

My father was in a coma for two days before he awoke. He woke up confused and disoriented and pulled out his IVs and catheters in an effort to escape. It took four security guards to restrain him and strap him down to his stretcher. When I was allowed to visit him, he was heavily medicated and an indication of the previous struggle was obvious: leather restraints tied to the gurney. The medication caused my father to be paranoid and delusional. He would whisper in my ear to help him escape, believing the nurses and doctors had ill intentions for him. This was a frightening and confusing time for me. This was not my father. I had no way to conceptualize what was happening in this situation. But after a month in intensive care and several more weeks in the hospital, my father came home.

He decided to return to work after only a few weeks. His strong work ethic and equally stubborn nature, simultaneously his greatest strengths and greatest weaknesses, motivated this quick return. He was supposed to quit smoking at the suggestion of his doctor and began using nicotine gum and patches. As far as I knew, he was abstaining from cigarettes. When we were playing basketball one day, a pack of cigarettes fell out of his sock. I was furious. I felt betrayed. After everything my family had gone through with his heart attack, I could not understand why he would begin smoking again.

I threw the basketball at him and ran inside to tell on him to my mother. My father began traveling out of town to auto auctions for his work. These business trips took him away from home ten to fifteen days out of the month. He spent the majority of his time in Albuquerque, New Mexico, but also traveled to Texas and New Jersey every month. My dad purchased tickets to the 1996 World Cup, which was being held in Dallas, Texas. The match was between Argentina and Bulgaria and I was rooting for Argentina. When the morning of the match came, sitting in the Howard Johnson Hotel in Dallas, the local news announced that the star player, Francisco Maradona, had tested positive for cocaine and was disqualified from participating in the match. I was devastated. This was a once in a lifetime opportunity to see my soccer idol play in the World Cup and he would not be allowed in the game for using a drug that was completely foreign to me.

Despite this disappointment, we went to the game and security was nothing like I had ever seen. Soccer is known for its excessively passionate fans and riots are common. No purses, coolers, bags, or water bottles were allowed inside the arena. All of the water fountains had been turned off and as it was a July afternoon in Dallas, the heat was unbearable. We purchased four-dollar water bottles before finding our seats. The game was fun, but Bulgaria won and I knew it was because Argentina's star player had not been allowed to play. This vacation was simply one of the many memorable family experiences I was privileged to have while growing up.

DISRUPTION

"You must be getting pretty good at that thing," commented my father with a gesture towards my snowboard. He was sitting in the dining room with my mother playing Yahtzee, their nightly ritual. I was in eighth grade and had begun snowboarding during the school year. My school had a program called Ski Blitz that allowed students to take a bus to Brighton Ski resort after school and snowboard or ski for several hours.

I had been preparing my snowboarding gear in the dining room when my father made his remark. These final words of his would haunt me for years to come.

January 17, 1997. The turning point of my life. My mother and I had gone to the airport to pick up my father from a recent trip to Albuquerque. We waited at his terminal, watching as all of the passengers exited the plane. He was not among them. My mother looked concerned. I turned to her and suggested that perhaps he had simply taken another flight. My dad would frequently take alternate flights when the airlines had overbooked to receive the benefits offered by the airlines. It seemed reasonable to me that he had could have just taken another flight, but my mother remained unrelieved.

When we arrived back home I went to hang out with my best friend, Jordan, and our other friend, Chris. As we walked to Chris's house, I explained to my friends how worried my mom had been at the airport and how I thought she was acting ridiculous. Inside I was wondering what had caused her to be so alarmed.

We had only been at Chris's for a few minutes when there was a knock at the door. I was in the kitchen, but walked to the top of the stairs right as Chris opened the door. It was Jordan's mother, Sheila. She was crying and having a difficult time keeping her composure. She had been a close family friend for years and it was alarming to see her so distraught. She finally managed to look at me and say, "Aaron, you need to come with me." My heart sank. My emotional state shifted. I could hardly move. She repeated herself.

As we drove in the car, Sheila continued crying and said nothing. She didn't need to say anything. I already knew what was happening on some level, but I remained in a daze the whole ride home. Sheila could barely control herself. She couldn't stop crying, wasn't saying anything to me, couldn't even look at me. There were perhaps a hundred yards between Chris's house and mine, but it seemed to take a year before we finally pulled in the driveway. I ran into the house to find Sheila's husband, Terry, there with my mom. They were both crying. My mother grabbed me and said, "Dad had another heart attack. He didn't make it this time, honey." My whole world went numb.

This single event would change my life

DIFFERENT WORLD

I remember little of the funeral. I had detached from the world and was hiding. Everything had moved to the recesses of my mind. I retreated deep within myself. My dad's viewing produced businessmen in flashy cars. Some I recognized; most I did not. My father had died in his hotel room in Albuquerque while on a business trip and was found in the morning by the maids. I hated all of these men. I hated them for showing up to his viewing in their fancy cars and leather jackets, for socializing as if it were a conference. I remember hating them.

The actual funeral services are lost in my memory; I was sitting in the front row, yet I remember nothing. I was lost. The world looked dim. It was as if someone had turned a dimmer switch and my vision had become dull and glum. I felt all alone.

My schoolwork was the first to suffer. I began acting up in class and could often be found in after school detention. I was kicked out of one of my science classes because of my erratic and disruptive behavior, talking back to the teacher and showing a complete disregard for learning. I was eventually transferred to another class. The teacher simply could not deal with me anymore. I subsequently dropped out of all my advanced classes.

I didn't want to be an advanced student. I didn't want to excel anymore. I didn't want to be around positive students who were so excited about life. I had lost all sense of meaning. My life had changed. My family's life was forced to change. My mother had no choice but to obtain employment and began working full-time at Salt Lake Community College.

I joined a band the summer between ninth and tenth grade. From there I developed a group of acquaintances and approached my first day of high school already attached to a less than favorable social group. My first day of high school came and many of these acquaintances decided to skip that day. They reasoned that there is so much confusion on the first day that no one would notice anyway. I rarely attended a full day of school after that. On one particular day, I left school with a group of peers to buy marijuana and get high. I had smoked marijuana on a few other occasions, always inconsequential, recreational, with other curious teens that had little experience with drugs. This time was different. This time we smoked all day and failed to attend any of our classes. I liked this. I found this very appealing; drowning my feelings in intoxication, leaving school behind, avoiding social interactions wherever possible. Getting high provided an avenue to avoid my feelings. I was losing all feeling. I was always high, I was depressed, and I hated talking to anyone. My silence kept me safe; getting high kept me safe. The pain I felt was always near the surface, tears on the verge of spilling out, but getting high subdued the pain. Using drugs and reusing to communicate with anyone were the only ways I knew how to cope. I may have spoken only a few thousand words during my sophomore year.

As my drug use progressed, I began experimenting with different kinds of drugs. Mostly hallucinogens, but also some cocaine. I began selling drugs in an effort to make money to purchase more drugs, but found that even at this stage I used too much to make any money. I was forced to seek alternate methods to support my habit: Discovery of silver bullion in which my father had invested provided one such method. I couldn't help myself. It was as if I had lost all control. Every time I snuck into the garage to the place where the silver had been hidden, I was consumed with guilt, as if my father was watching me. But I couldn't help myself. I continued selling the silver bullion until there was none left. I sold $17,000 worth of silver to support my drug use for six months of my sophomore year.

The only positive activity I engaged in during high school was boxing. My father had boxed at a semiprofessional level in Boston and I had always wanted to get involved. He discouraged me due to the many less than favorable people involved in the sport, but boxing became an oasis of sorts for me. Although my drug use did not subside, I worked out every day in preparation for my first fight.

My first fight was held in Tooele, Utah. I was fifteen years old. I was beaten badly during the first round, sustaining a black eye and accompanying blurry vision. But then halfway through the fight, something inside of me kicked in and I began to turn the fight around. I was bloodying the other fighter, I was winning, I was good, I was tough. In that moment, I felt more alive than I had since my father's death. This was a feeling I could only recreate while boxing.

Junior year proved to be much the same as my sophomore year: getting in fights, getting high, disrupting class, skipping class, and more getting high. I had to meet with the administration for missing more than half of my classes and was suspended multiple times for confrontations and fights. By my senior year, I had developed a reputation for violence. During one such incident, another classmate initiated an argument with me and the situation quickly spiraled out of control. I felt like a third party watching myself as I assaulted this classmate, controlled by some outside force as I pushed him to the ground and kicked him multiple times in the head. I was suspended and he ended up in a neck brace. The sadness I had turned inwards could no longer be contained and was bursting like a water pipe, explosions of anger and violence occurring at times without provocation or pattern.

I received a safe school violation for attacking my classmate and was unable to attend any school within my district. The only option remaining was to attend an alternate high school program once a week where I completed asinine packets for school credit. My various suspensions had caused me to fall significantly behind and I needed to complete an inordinate amount of packets to make up the credits in order to graduate high school on schedule. I was completely unmotivated to graduate, but two hours of a weekly class with nothing else to do coupled with my academic ability allowed me to complete enough packets to get back on course to graduate. It was a joke how easily I was able to get caught up on credits.

Having no classes to attend and being at home during the day only perpetuated my substance abuse and resulting criminal activity. I began selling more drugs to support my habit and connected with multiple gangs in order to access these drugs: Piru Original Gangsters (POG), West Side Crips, and Gangster Disciples (GD). Because of friends and acquaintances of mine who were involved with gangs, I was treated like an honorary gang member who was never jumped in, but was accepted nonetheless. I was creating a framework for a career in crime and drugs, all driven by my compulsion to use drugs as often as possible.

My life seemed to transform quickly. I had separated from the world and no longer found comfort from considering myself part of the world. I began wearing bright colors and loved wearing primarily red, the gang color of the Blood gang, POG. It was like the bright frogs in South

America whose colors are a signal to predators to stay away due to their posion. For me, bright colors and a thousand yard stare accomplished the same effect. The signal I was sending to people was clear: stay away, I am toxic. This helped perpetuate my self-imposed isolation from other human beings and alienation from a world that felt so cruel.

I eventually decided to appeal my suspension to the school district disciplinary board. When I arrived in front of the board, I discovered that one of the members was an administrator from my junior high who had met with me regarding some of behavioral issues in ninth grade. After three years, it seemed an uncanny coincidence. My appeal was denied, but I was authorized to return to school for the final semester of my senior year.

I graduated from Taylorsville High School in June of 2000. Like the packets I had to complete to get there, graduation was a joke. My lack of attendance should have excluded me from graduating and the only people who applauded when I received my diploma consisted of people I used drugs with. I was high during the graduation; a typically memorable ceremony was meaningless to me. I was out of touch. My classmates wore smiles on their faces, ecstatic about the momentous occasion in their lives and excited about the future. I was indifferent to the event. I was dying on the inside.

PROGRESSION

Graduation raised my drug use to a whole new level. I was still selling drugs, but began pawning items from my mother's house as well to support my habit. I sold televisions, stereos, cameras, guns, jewelry, everything in the house of any value in a desperate effort to finance my increasingly expensive drug habit.

Knowing my mother would often put money in books, I was searching for some of this hidden money when I stumbled upon a fake book filled with nearly seven thousand dollars. Every hundred-dollar bill was the old design. Based on the time of my father's death, I realized he must have hidden this money. Opening the book brought a flood of emotions. This hiding spot had been privy to only my father and now the contents inside were being exposed for the first time in years like a time capsule.

I immediately went to the Piru Original Gangsters to purchase a couple thousand dollars worth of marijuana and hundreds of ecstasy tablets. I purchased a scale, a pager, and a nine-millimeter handgun and, like my drug use, I began selling drugs at a whole new level. Because my network within the drug world was so vast, I was quickly able to develop a wide customer base.

For the first time in years, I felt free of addiction. I no longer had to steal money or wait for drugs; they were readily available to me. The reality of my situation escaped me: I was only digging myself deeper into the trenches and losing any real ability to make choices. Drugs were dictating my choices. I had to get high as soon as I woke up in the morning before any other activity. Selling drugs to others would completely consume the rest of my day.

Within a year after high school, three people I had gone to both junior high and high school with died within a week of each other. Rob had been a true entrepreneur. He spent an entire school year in junior high selling caramel apple suckers to make enough money to buy a drum set. I would play drums for his band on occasion. He died falling off a cliff. He had been hiking late at night after a rave, high on ecstasy. The next was my childhood friend, Chris Hall, the friend whose house I was at when I heard the news of my father's death. Chris was a black belt in Karate and would break pieces of wood for show and tell in elementary school. He crashed into a power pole going eighty miles an hour in the middle of the night. It is likely he was intoxicated. Paul was found hanging from the ceiling in his garage. Toxicology reports indicated alcohol in his system. This string of events was tragic, painful, eye opening, but had no effect on my drug use. I couldn't even attend Chris's viewing or funeral without using a considerable amount of drugs.

Shortly after these events, I went to Las Vegas with a group of friends and brought some cocaine with me. I had good connections for obtaining cocaine because of all the gangs I interacted with, specifically the Pirus, who made the majority of their income from this lucrative trade of poison. My friends and I liked the cocaine so much, we decided to get more as soon as we returned to Salt Lake City. Cocaine seemed to give me an energy and social aptitude I had lacked for many years. I had found a new drug of choice. I quickly developed a habit costing two hundred dollars a day.

In order to maintain my habit, I became the middleman for many people, charging a higher price for the drugs as well as taking some of the drugs for my troubles. This was not enough. I finally began simply taking people's money and giving them nothing in return. Given my reputation, there was nothing they dared to do. As I ran out of people to rob, I began stealing from my mother again. Cocaine had a grip on me I had never felt with any other drug. My only focus was on obtaining more drugs. I would become physically sick when I ran out; the withdrawal symptoms only encouraged me to obtain more.

I began to commit forgery. I stole, forged, and cashed checks from my mother and even activated a credit card under her name while pretending to be a female to the operator. My mother could easily have pressed charges and landed me in prison for countless years. To this day, I'm not sure why she didn't. In the act of committing these crimes, I seemed to lack the ability to refrain regardless of the potential consequences. The compulsion for drugs was too great.

I was quickly running out of options for obtaining money, but my need for cocaine was only increasing. I began burglarizing houses, especially houses where I would party and then wait for everyone to fall asleep. I was like a vulture. One such party resulted in detectives opening a case for grand theft; the stolen items included a Tahitian pearl necklace, a baguette diamond necklace, and several thousand dollars worth of additional items. I was the main suspect. The detectives eventually had to close the case due to lack of evidence.

Next I was contacted for theft of a firearm in another county. I was asked to answer questions regarding the case, but refused based on my inability to travel. I was never bothered again, as there was insufficient evidence to charge me. I was hardly fazed by these encounters with law enforcement. I was only concerned about continuing to obtain cocaine on a daily basis. I could see my life spiraling downwards, as if from the view of a third person, like I was only observing; I had no real control.

I would begin to get cranky and sick whenever I went without drugs. I would binge on large amounts of candy in order to alleviate the withdrawals. Eating that much sugar would recreate a smaller version of the monstrous dopamine spikes produced by drugs. On a few occasions, I ate so many sweets I subsequently puked. I intellectually knew my situation had become absolutely ridiculous, but I couldn't quit.

After a year of continuous cocaine use, my sinuses began suffering. I would have a constant bloody nose throughout the day and often find large pieces of cartilage in my Tissues after blowing my nose. My nasal cavity had deteriorated so much I could shine a flashlight in one nostril and see the light in the other. My sinuses were often so inflamed I couldn't even snort any cocaine without blowing my nose violently multiple times and then quickly sniffing the drug. Once while looking down at cartilage in my hand and a line of cocaine on the counter, I wondered if I was causing irreparable damage. I quickly dismissed the thought with a toss of the cartilage and proceeded to blow my nose and take the line. I wasn't done yet.

My main connection for cocaine was an affiliate of the Pirus. He had been connecting a guy with a kilo a week. The kilos were coming from the Mexican Mafia, a street gang and drug cartel. Many were suspicious of this guy. One of the weekly buys was taking place when a Gangster Disciple grabbed a shotgun in the room and robbed both parties. The Mexican Mafia member open fired on him as he ran from the house, but missed. It turned out that the guy buying the cocaine was an undercover agent for the FBI. My drug dealer now had the heat of the FBI and the Mexican Mafia who wanted their money back. This would bring heat to all members of these gangs and their affiliates.

It was all like a dream I would forget immediately after it happened. I simply continued spending my days getting money, getting high, and frequenting houses with drugs and crimes.

One week later, after being up for three days straight, I was pulled over by the Drug Task Force while leaving another dealer's house. I had cocaine hidden in my sock—I was positive I was going to be arrested. I became suddenly calm. I didn't have a chance and I knew it. I decided to patronize the police and be sarcastically helpful in my sleep-deprived delirium. They brought a K9 unit onto the scene to search my car while another officer searched me. They turned up nothing and I was allowed to return to continue destroying my life.

At one point, I decided to leave home and use some backpacking gear to live outside. Fighting with my mother about being gone for days and trying to hide my drug use had become too much trouble. I made the conscious choice to be homeless. The choice was neither profound nor necessitated by circumstance. I simply decided to become homeless. I began sleeping near my drug dealer's house in bushes or behind the storage shed of a local church. The neighborhood was in an expensive area of town and I would often find myself wandering in the middle of the night among multi-million dollar homes. I was probably the only homeless man living within five miles!

I ended up burning all of my bridges. No one wanted to purchase cocaine from me. Even dealers hated selling to me at this point. My behavior was erratic. I would show up at dealer's doors at all hours unannounced with ridiculous items to trade for drugs. I was a complete fiend. As my ability to score cocaine became more difficult, some of the guys I used with began using methamphetamine. The decision was simple; I made the transition.

INSANITY

High school was spent smoking marijuana, drinking alcohol, whatever I could get my hands on at the time and lots of it. Cocaine was different. I only spent a year on cocaine. It didn't last very long. I was always needing more and more and more. But meth, meth was exciting. Meth was fast-paced, meth was reckless, meth was erratic. Just like me.

I began meeting many new people as I became quickly entrenched in the methamphetamine scene. I was forced to hook up with different gangs since the gangs I had previously dealt with didn't use or sell meth. The first gangs I connected with were the Vigil Family (VGL) and the Vario Loco Town (VLT).

One day at a VLT house, a gang member pulled out a Salt Lake City PD badge that they used for robberies. I mentioned a sheriff badge I had obtained during a burglary from my cocaine days and naturally they wanted to buy it. I traded the badge for fifty dollars worth of methamphetamine. The seriousness of the stolen badge eluded me, not to mention the insignificant amount of drugs I was given. But I couldn't seem to conceptualize things that way—I was getting more drugs and that seemed to be all that mattered.

I loved the fast-paced lifestyle in this drug scene. I loved only sleeping every few days. My reckless attitude and disregard for the law allowed me to work my way up the ranks and I began hanging out with meth cooks, the ones who actually manufactured the drugs. As I was no longer staying at my mother's house, I would only stop by in order to retrieve clean clothes. I carried around an army issue duffel bag and traveled all over the city, sleeping different places every night. I never slept in a bed and I was always fully clothed in order to quickly exit the highly volatile dwellings I frequented.

It was during this time period I began to experience paranoia and delusions due to the combination of sleep deprivation, drug use, and minimal food intake. Going days without food or sleep provided ideal conditions for drug-induced paranoia. I began experiencing delusions of reference, believing that cars or other inanimate objects were watching and that everyone was talking about me.

One house I would stay at occasionally was a historic house built by Mormon polygamists. There was a tunnel system that connected it with its three neighboring houses, which had likely been built as an escape route for the original tenants. Polygamists had come to Utah to avoid persecution and often built such escape tunnels into their houses. The tunnels were now being used to manufacture methamphetamine. The crawl space should have been covered in cobwebs, but instead there was a vacant, sterile feel to the space. Insects couldn't survive the toxic atmosphere created by the noxious methamphetamine smoke, yet we were directly above it.

I eventually started hanging out with different motorcycle gangs, as they were some of the main players in manufacturing and selling methamphetamine. At this point, my life took a clear turn for the worse— these were criminal organizations dedicated purely to illegal activities. And yet I didn't care. I met a girl named Susan at one of these biker gang houses and she became a perfect partner in crime. She loved to steal, use drugs all day, and was a wanderer like me.

I managed to score a hotel room through some bikers while Susan managed to come up with a few thousand dollars. We stayed in one hotel and the bikers stayed in the next hotel over. Susan had gone to their hotel to buy some stolen checks and merchandise when I fell asleep. I awoke to a knock at the door. I looked through the peephole and saw a hotel employee there. I slowly opened the door.

"Put your hands up," someone said softly. A police officer had been hiding out of sight. He began questioning me about who had paid for the room, where everyone else was, and the name of the girl who was staying in the room with me. I honestly didn't know the answers to these questions. I didn't even know Susan's real name. I was eventually taken to the lobby where all the criminals were corralled.

The police had raided both rooms in an effort to take down an identity theft ring. The rooms had been paid for with fraudulent credit cards causing the raid. Because I possessed no illegal documents or drugs and hadn't paid for the hotel rooms, I was released. I walked outside with my army duffle bag in hand and took a transit train into the city.

I went to the north side of town to one of my regular stops, a house occupied by associates of prominent biker gangs. I would frequent this house to rest, score dope, and sell stolen merchandise. When I arrived, a phone message was waiting for me from Susan. She had left a message with the hotel and room number she was staying at. The occupants of the house were furious with me because they didn't trust Susan. In all reality, I didn't trust her either as it was very possible she had turned informant. I hardly knew Susan and the streets had taught me to despise snitches, but I decided to take the chance and go to her hotel anyway.

Susan had a room at a cheap hotel, a pocket full of money, and lots of drugs. It was good enough for me. We got high all night and continued well into the next day. When we needed to get more drugs, we headed to a hotel by Salt Lake International Airport to hook up. Drug users, traffickers, and dealers commonly used hotels as a forum for business transactions and residences. When we arrived at the room, I began to feel something was wrong. I had been up for seven days at this point, so it was hard to differentiate between reality and paranoia.

Someone suddenly came bursting into the room and yelled, "There are cops in the lobby!" The cops were apparently talking to some guy who was on his way to the room.

Susan and I bolted down the stairs and were about to exit the building when we noticed the fifteen police cars parked outside. Others were circling the building in an attempt to trap its inhabitants. We decided to make a run for it. We waited as one police car passed and then ran directly behind it before running to our car. The officer didn't stop; he must not have seen us. We ducked down and stayed hidden in our car for over two hours before driving away and ending up at the house on the north side. Susan was not allowed to stay and I spent the whole night lying awake.

The following morning, we received word that multiple people had been arrested at the hotel. I didn't care; I had escaped. I had been up for eight days by this point and was becoming increasingly tired and delusional. The meth in my system had postponed any physical fatigue, but I was coming down and I needed to stay awake. I decided to go for a walk to find something to burglarize for drug money.

The next thing I remember was sitting on the curb in front of a Maverick nearly half a mile away. I had blacked out. My ears were ringing and traffic sounds were alternating between really loud and ultra soft. I had a difficult time focusing my eyes and everything appeared very bright. My body was shutting down and my sensory perception was all out of whack. I recalled an argument I had with the inhabitants of the house on the north side, but it felt like a dream. I began making my way back to the house.

I was met by a group of furious individuals for the scene I apparently had caused. They told me I had been yelling, drawing attention to the house. I was prohibited from any further drug use until I slept. It was as if I had been a bad little boy and was being put in criminal timeout!

When I woke up the next day, it started all over again, getting high and planning ways to score more drugs. This is when I met Jesse Cochran. He was in the process of scoring us some drugs, but I was struck by his similarity to me. He was around my age and on a similar path of self-destruction. He was wild, lost, but somewhere underneath there existed a good person. I would encounter Jesse many times over the next few years, each time having lost more and more of the part of himself that was good. Just like me.

LOST

It didn't take long for me to become lost in meth, lost in the scene, lost in the world, lost in my addiction. I was lost. I was completely out of place hanging around bikers that were typically twice my age and had racial ideologies in complete opposition to my own. They believed that white people were superior, that people of color were lesser human beings, and used pejorative language referring to people of other ethnicities.

Before entering the meth scene, my time had been spent with gangs of various ethnicities. I enjoyed wearing bright colors and listening to rap music. This caused many of those around me to have contempt for me. I would often encounter comments that were indirectly threatening, but due to my reputation, few people directly insulted me. My fear, coupled with drug-induced paranoia, led me to believe I needed another weapon. I contacted an old friend and purchased a handgun I had sold to him a few years previous.

After purchasing the gun, I went to a house on the south side of Salt Lake to score some drugs. I would frequent this house when I needed to get more drugs or a place to crash. The Sundowners, a Utah based motorcycle gang, owned this house. When I arrived, Stevie, a girl approximately my age, greeted me at the door. She was a well-known methamphetamine cook and related to members of the Hells Angels. She was currently on the run due to recent drug raids where she was the primary target. She was on her way to meet someone at the closest gas station and bring him back to the house. Needing someone to walk with her, I quickly obliged. We met a guy nicknamed Smiley and got into his car to drive back to the house. He parked the car and we began getting out when an SUV and a truck screeched in behind us and a group of men jumped out of the vehicles. They were dressed in leather vests, carrying bats, poles, and had menacing glares. Fear consumed my consciousness, fear of what I might be capable of. I had the pistol I had purchased earlier tucked in my belt and I was fully prepared to use it. These men did not frighten me, but the realization of how quickly this situation could escalate was worrisome. Even with a weapon, I felt helpless to control the chaos that would potentially ensue if the situation got out of control.

The men proceeded to surround Smiley and harass him regarding some incident that had occurred the previous day. A few of the men glanced at me with apprehension. I was dressed in gang attire, smoking a cigarette, and appeared completely unaffected by what was going on around me. One man began to antagonize me, asking questions about Smiley and attempting to intimidate me.

"Look, I am just in the car. I've never met him. Do I look like I'm a biker?" I asked with a tone of disrespect. His response could have led to a very bad altercation, but he simply turned away. His gut must have told him to disregard me, that there was some unknown variable about me that he simply didn't want to engage. These guys were members of a white supremacist gang, the Silent Arian Warriors (SAW), whereas Smiley had ties to a rival gang of sorts, the Soldiers of Arian Culture (SAC), a different white supremacist gang.

I made my way back inside the Sundowners' house after everyone dispersed. A man came rushing into the house looking disgruntled and agitated. He had somehow heard that members of SAW had just been outside the house. This man was a general of the Fourth Reich, a local white supremacist gang that had primary control of the Utah State Prison culture. Recent drug busts and federal arrests had created a shifting in balance. There was a war going on between white supremacist gangs, motorcycle gangs, and law enforcement. I had managed to find myself right in the middle. I felt like I was in a foreign country. The culture and belief system were completely different than my own and here I was in the middle of their civil war.

I decided it was best to leave the area and headed back to the house on the North Side to avoid the chaotic mess. I was not greeted with the normal welcome I had come to expect. They had caught wind of what had transpired at the Sundowners' house and everyone was visibly on edge. The criminal network could be amazing in this sense. Everyone at the house wanted to keep a low profile and no one was selling any dope that day.

With nowhere else to go, I went back to the Sundowners' house hoping somebody would be willing to hook me up with some dope. Civil war aside, I was more than willing to walk back into the war zone to obtain more drugs. I had already been up for several days and needed to be recharged. When I arrived, nobody had any drugs to sell, but Stevie said she could go and get some. When she received a phone call from the place she had recently stayed at informing her it had been raided, it became evident that law enforcement was still looking for her. She seemed only slightly concerned and left to score the dope anyway.

Only a few minutes after her departure, a knock came from the front of the house. I opened the door to find myself face to face with five federal marshals in black attire. My heart sank. With a gun in my waistband, I immediately saw prison in my near future.

"Where's Stevie?" one of the marshals asked. Knowing my situation was hopeless, I settled into the calm I always seemed to find in such situations and decided to antagonize the federal marshals.

"Oh, she already left. She knew y'all were on the way," I flippantly responded. This was the wrong thing to say. I was ordered back inside the house where another group of marshals came rushing into the room after securing the back portion of the house. They began running all of our identification to see if any of us were wanted, but they were stopped short. A phone call drew them out of the house and into their black Dodge Durango's, leaving me behind in a state of disbelief.

After this event, I decided to stay away from the Sundowners' house for a while and headed to the North Side to stay for a few days. The day after my arrival, the Salt Lake Police Task Force raided the house and questioned me about my gang affiliation and criminal past. They were looking for a man named Brett, one of the worst souls I have ever encountered in my life. I knew enough about him to know he was a complete sociopath.

I was beginning to feel more and more uneasy wherever I went because of the constant police harassment and the undesirable characters I always managed to find myself around. It had been months since I had slept in an actual bed and my mind and body were starting to feel the wear and tear. I started obtaining pure methamphetamine directly from a manufacturer that lived in an apartment complex called the Way Fares Inn. It was clearly evident that dope was cooked in this apartment: glassware was drying on a plastic rack where most people dry their dishes, vials and condensers were located throughout the rooms, and five gallon buckets were filled with pure methamphetamine. I couldn't help but think about how many unassuming neighbors were breathing in the toxic fumes.

To get the pure meth, I started buying blue iodine for the cook at the Way Fares Inn and ephedrine for another cook. Knowing it could cause unwanted attention, the cooks never purchased the ephedrine or blue iodine themselves. Blue iodine was especially hard to come by and I had to but it at a business named the Ball &Feed. This was an agricultural store that sold the chemical for prevention of hoof rot in cattle and horses. Because blue iodine was a federally monitored chemical, the business required identification in order to enter the data into their database.

I had been purchasing ephedrine for months and blue iodine for a slightly shorter amount of time when I heard about two men who had been indicted on federal cases for purchasing the iodine. The cases involved the manufacturing of meth. I quickly ceased purchasing these chemicals as a result of the indictments.

I began frequenting the Sundowners' house again and arrived there one night with hundreds of dollars worth of drugs I had stolen from someone else. I met a man I had never seen before, but I immediately disliked him. Something wasn't right, something wasn't right about him and I could feel it. He started drilling me with questions: "Do you have any dope? Can you get some?" He was supposed to be going with one of the Sundowners to Wendover the next morning to score a kilo of cocaine, but he was trying to spend all of his money that night. It didn't seem right. With all of the recent events involving police coupled with my drug use and lack of sleep, I was jumping out of my skin. My internal warning meters were off the charts and I knew I had to get out of there. I announced I was going to buy some cigarettes and would be right back. I ran into the darkness with a pistol and a pocketful of drugs at two in the morning. It wasn't a particularly brilliant plan, as the house was right next to the Salt Lake Police Station, but I didn't care. I had to get away from there. I made the journey all the way to the north side and was warmly welcomed when I displayed the amount of drugs I possessed. The next day, I discovered that the suspicious man was an informant for some law enforcement agency. The Sundowner that had traveled with him to Wendover was sitting in a jail in Nevada on federal charges. I could easily have wound up in federal prison with the amount of drugs I had in my possession along with the handgun. Another close call.

I began hanging out at the house on the north side again, getting high, stealing, using drugs, and looking for more. After several days of this,

an acquaintance came over with a weird request— a girl's mother that
he knew needed us to haul off some garbage in his truck. With nothing
better to do, I agreed to go along. We picked up the girl and headed to the
eastern edge of South Salt Lake. The girl borrowed my friend's phone to
call her mother for directions, but began making a series of phone calls.
My internal warning meters went crazy again. I asked to see the phone,
saying I needed to make a call. She proceeded to delete all of the numbers
she had dialed with alarming speed instead of handing the phone over. I
was totally freaked out and quickly said, "Pull the car over. I need a drink."
The girl immediately objected, arguing that we were almost there anyway.
I looked my friend in the eyes and said, "Pull the car over now. I need
a drink." We pulled into a Maverick gas station. I jumped out of the
vehicle and headed straight for the garbage can. As hastily as I could,
I dumped two methamphetamine pipes and twenty bags full of meth
residue I had been saving into the garbage can. I walked back to the car
and hopped in while the girl talked on the phone getting directions to
the house. I was unsure as to why she didn't know how to get to her
mother's house, but I was sure we were being set up.

When we got to the house, a series of suspicious looking cars were
parked along the street. "This isn't right, man," I whispered to my
friend. "Every car on the street has three antennas." He assured me that
everything was cool.

We ended up in the backyard and emptied out nine garbage cans. We
pulled back to the front of the house and waited for the girl to come out.
By this point, my friend was also alarmed. We stepped outside to have
a cigarette. "Well, I am pretty sure we have been set up," I said almost off-
handedly. "We may have just hauled off a meth lab, but if we're tripping,
then we need to get some sleep." We contemplated dumping all of the
trash in the middle of the street and leaving the girl there, but we decided

that was ridiculous. We couldn't just dump the garbage in the middle of the street, so we came to the conclusion that we were just being paranoid from the drugs and sleep deprivation. When the girl finally came out, we decided to leave and hope for the best.

"We're being pulled over," my friend said after driving for a minute. I thought he was joking, but when I looked in the rearview mirror, I realized we had made a mistake and that our instincts had been right. The agents came to car door, one with a goatee like ZZ Top and both with long hair, dressed like they belonged at a rock concert. They were undercover Drug Enforcement Agency (DEA) agents. We were extracted from the car and watched as the agents meticulously searched the truck and the garbage. My friend was arrested for a bench warrant issued by a judge for being absent in court and I was allowed to drive the truck away. The agents must have pulled us over in hopes of finding drugs to gain a search warrant for the house. They came up empty handed. However, within a few weeks, both the man and woman at the house were arrested for operating a clandestine methamphetamine laboratory and were eventually sentenced to federal prison. He got eleven years and she got seventeen.

This encounter didn't even deter me for more than a few hours. The need to obtain more drugs was always foremost in my thoughts. Later that night, after bailing my friend out of jail, I found myself at an abandoned house "pulling ephedrine." This was the method for getting ephedrine out of cold medicine with the intent of producing meth. It seemed my compulsion to use drugs always outweighed my ability to make good decisions.

I went to the Sundowners' house one last time. I had been up for five days and was looking to score. When I arrived at the house, I immediately sensed the tension and animosity that was focused towards me. The nonverbal cues were enough to suggest that if I had stayed there, the men would have assaulted me. I left there with the knowledge that I would never go back again and headed to the Golden Glove State Championships. Even though I was scheduled to fight that night, I had intended on getting high instead. Circumstance led me back to the fight. I had been under the influence for all of my previous fights, but this time I had been up for five days and should not have been fighting. I was winning the fight initially, but halfway through the third round I got in trouble. I quit for the first and last time ever in the ring.

ELEMENTS

There was too much chaos, too much confusion. Moving from house to house, dodging questions from my mother, the paranoia, the insecurity, the chaos, it had all simply become too much. I made a decision: I was literally going to live on the streets. I had spent some time living on the streets when I was using cocaine and it was absolutely horrible, but I no longer felt safe anywhere. So much had occurred in the past five months, so much tumult and turmoil. The run-ins with the DEA, with Federal Marshals, and with the task force had all taken place in the previous month alone. All of these events combined with my drug use produced a consuming paranoia. I was constantly looking over my shoulder and feeling like everything was closing in on me. I had sold my gun to have some extra cash and instead carried two large pocketknives for weapons. Living on the streets among the chronically homeless requires entering a completely different world. Most members of the homeless community suffer from substance abuse and mental health problems; I fit right in with them. Heavy drug use often results in drug-induced psychosis, a temporary form of mental illness. Alleviation of this psychosis required abstinence from drugs. One of the well-known gathering places for homeless people and illicit drug use in Salt Lake City is Pioneer Park. I would often walk through this park to get to a drug dealer's house. I became homeless to avoid the chaos of my life, but I seemed to be drawn toward it. Rather than circumvent the park, I always chose to walk right through it. It was as if I was magnetically drawn to unhealthy people. When a pair of homeless men walked by me one evening, one of them turned and squawked at me like a chicken. I should have simply kept walking. There were two of them and they were clearly not mentally stable. Instead, I engaged in a verbal confrontation with them, drawing on my street pride and instinctually pulling out both of my knives to threaten them. Clearly I was more unstable than the other two. I recognized that I was becoming increasingly dangerous to both others and myself. My inability to control myself was troubling because I realized I was capable of getting myself into a world of trouble.

I continued living outside even as the weather grew colder. On one particular evening, I was trying to sleep between two abandoned buildings, but I was unable to fall asleep due to the high concentration of homeless people walking by. I didn't trust homeless people primarily because I knew they shouldn't be trusted if they were as troubled as me. I often managed to find some warmth in parking garages. On blistering cold evenings, I would travel to a mall that was still under construction. My clothing was always substandard for the weather. I would ride the parking garage elevators while avoiding the night security for hours in attempts to stay warm.

The reality of my situation hit me on Christmas Day that year. The streets were empty, as people were enjoying the holiday with their loved ones, and I was alone in the nightmare I had managed to create for myself. There was a blizzard outside and I was sure I would freeze to death. I made my way to the house on the north side to get out of the storm, but I was not welcome that day. Even the bikers and drug dealers had family members coming over and the house was off-limits to a junkie like me. I wasn't interested in being with my family, so I was stuck out in the cold. I had successfully alienated myself from the world. Eventually I managed to find a building in downtown Salt Lake City that had an architecturally masterful façade. I took refuge in a place between the glass and a support beam that created a geometrical illusion.

I walked countless miles during my time outdoors. On weekends, kids my age were hanging out at the nightclubs and restaurants of downtown while I was walking around with a huge backpack on my shoulders. We were living in two different worlds that occupied the same time and space. They had smiles on their faces, the men flirting with the women, the women laughing with their friends. All I could focus on was getting high. Their scene was completely foreign to me.

One night, an argument broke out in front of a club I happened to be walking by. Approximately twenty guys, likely gang members, were getting increasingly agitated amongst themselves and security was not capable of dealing with the situation. One of the men threw a landscaping boulder threw the front window and the others followed suit. The men tried to disperse after breaking all the windows, but police officers had already set up a perimeter and began tackling and arresting the men. As I stood and watched the scene, I was not even regarded as a suspect. My backpack and homeless attire ruled me out. One cop seemed to glance at me momentarily like I was a mirage flickering in and out of focus, but then his attention was back to the scene. I was not unlike a condemned house: I only attracted transients and was an eyesore that everyone else attempted to ignore.

COCKROACHES

I eventually went back to the house on the north side. My mind and body were withered from the continual movement and consistent exposure to the elements. I just needed a place to crash for the night. The lady who sold drugs there, Linda, offered to let me sleep in her room. As the main drug distributor in the house, she never slept alone in her room to avoid theft. Her boyfriend was in jail and she figured I would be helpful in keeping an eye on her drugs.

She gave me a pair of shorts and I fell asleep as soon as my head hit the pillow. It was the first time in nine months I had worn pajamas and slept in a bed. I may never have rested so well in all my life. I awoke feeling refreshed and wishing I could continue staying in this room. The room felt like an oasis placed to help and energize travelers making their treacherous journeys across the desert.

The members of the house decided I needed a place to stay. They allowed me to sleep on an abandoned couch in the garage; this was the place I called home. There were cockroaches all over the garage and in the house itself. Most of the houses where I stayed were infested with cockroaches. In nature, cockroaches are typically found in caves where they feast on bat guano. While this poor excuse for a dwelling wasn't covered in bat feces, it was unsanitary enough for the cockroaches to flourish.

I would often see cockroaches scampering around the garage, especially at night when hundreds would make their way across the floor and walls. I woke up suddenly one night, upright in a chair and holding a methamphetamine pipe with cockroaches crawling all over me. I swatted the cockroaches off of me and began hitting the pipe. I was trying to figure out how I could have fallen asleep with a pipe fully loaded in my hand. The body shuts down when deprived of sleep for too long and it is not uncommon to wake up holding things. It can be very disorienting, waking in strange places, fully clothed, recognizing that your body has shut down in the middle of task, but having no recollection or concept of the amount of time that has elapsed.

Although this house was not primarily used to cook methamphetamine, I suspected drugs were manufactured here on occasion based on the familiar telltale signs. When a batch of dope is being cooked, the air begins to appear foggy to those in close proximity due to the excessive toxins in the air. I began experiencing this one evening as at least three hundred cockroaches simultaneously made their way in a straight line out of the house through a crack in the door. I was delirious and decided to make a smart comment despite the potential negative consequences. "I wonder what they know that we don't," I remarked nonchalantly. Although the manufacturing of meth at this location was extremely covert, everyone in the room burst into immediate laughter.

While living in the garage, a girl named Crystal began hanging out around the house. Most of the people I interacted with from day to day were fifteen to twenty years older than me. It was oddly comforting to have someone from my generation around. Crystal was a lost soul like me, wild and operating from a fatalistic view of life. Finding others like me, individuals stuck in this world of despair, brought me a fleeting solace. This was one of the few human connections I made during this period of my life. Crystal and I shared some moments of intimacy in this world, brief moments of compassion that helped my spirit remain alive.

TIMEOUT

Linda had a nephew who had recently been released from jail after a long period of incarceration. He came to stay at the north side house and immediately began using methamphetamine and essentially running amuck. We started hanging out together in the garage, getting high and roaming various neighborhoods late at night. As a member of a local street gang, the Thirty-Third Street Lay Low Crips (LLC), blue was his clothing choice of color. We would antagonize each other for our choice of clothing color, his blue and mine red, but overall we were on the same page. We didn't care about anything apart from getting high.

On one particular night, we decided to go out into the neighborhood in search of anything we could steal from the cars along our way. Before leaving, Linda said to me, "Make sure and keep an eye on him." I left my marijuana pipe and both of my large pocketknives with Crystal, replacing the knives with a smaller version. I figured it was best to eliminate any illegal items that could be found in my possession.

Rob and I began roaming an area in Salt Lake City known at the Avenues, stealing compact discs, loose money, and other items of minimal value. We were by one of the oldest cemeteries in the city when Rob discovered a car with a nice stereo. I became the lookout nearly half a block away. Rob began dismantling the console when a man came charging out of the house in front of the car.

"What are you doing?" the man screamed. He was fairly large and athletic-looking and it was clear his intentions were dangerous.

Rob jumped out of the car and attempted to hop on his bicycle, but only managed to fall right over it. He stood up and fled down a side street on foot. I was already on my bike riding around the other side of the block. I contemplated leaving him, but heard Linda's voice in my head: "Make sure and keep an eye on him." I circled the block in time to see Rob get punched by the man before they disappeared behind some bushes. When I finally got to the location where I had seen them disappear, what I saw was shocking.

Rob was hanging horizontally on a rod iron fence, apparently impaled with his shirt torn and mouth bleeding. I jumped off my bike and ran towards the guy yelling, "What are you doing?" When he told me to mind my own business, I realized he was unaware of my involvement in the crime. I scared him off with a threat and began my attempt to get Rob off of the fence. He wouldn't budge. His belt had twisted tight around the pole, effectively securing him in place. When the police arrived, it took seven officers to get his feet back on the ground.

As the officers attempted to determine what had happened, I continued playing the innocent passerby while explaining my role in the situation. One witness even confirmed my story! Unfortunately, it was two in the morning, I was delirious from drugs and lack of sleep, and Rob's story didn't match mine. The officers quickly figured out what had really happened and I found myself on my way to jail for the first time.

The officer pulled into the jail through a back entrance. We arrived at fifty-foot gates that would have been menacing, perhaps even frightening, had I been in a proper state of mind. The officer spoke gruffly into an intercom: "Transporting one male." The gates swung open, as if in a warped welcome to us. This would not be the last time I entered by way of these gates.

The officer hastily escorted me through several sets of doors before he stopped and handcuffed me to a pole. I mentally prepared myself for the worst, as I no longer believed I would be treated as a human being. After being asked a series of questions by a nurse, I was eventually detached from the pole to begin my intake. A different officer told me to empty my pockets and then proceeded to search me. After a moment, the officer pulled a small bag of marijuana out of my pocket.

"Look what we have here. You're screwed now," he remarked off-handedly. I tried to explain to the officer that I didn't know the marijuana had been there, but it was wasted breath. I had been wearing the pants for several days and couldn't recall how long the marijuana had been in my pocket, but it really didn't matter. I was subsequently charged with vehicle burglary, possession of a burglary tool, possession of a dangerous weapon for the pocketknife, and smuggling contraband into a correctional facility. This final charge prevented me from being released from jail prior to appearing before a judge.

I simply didn't care. I had decided this was simply a part of the life I had chosen. I moved through the long and arduous booking process apathetically, although it was particularly tiring after being up for five days. When I was finally sent to a different room to be "dressed in," I was ordered to get stark naked, lift my feet, bend over, and spread my buttocks while an officer watched. I was given lice shampoo and ordered to shower and get dressed. The experience was intrusive, dehumanizing, but also somewhat sobering. I no longer had control of my life. Sadly, this was nothing new; I had surrendered control of my life to substances for years.

Next, placed in a holding cell. I was left to sleep on a cement floor for twenty-four hours. Next, transferred to quarantine, a temporary housing unit. Another twenty-four hours of sleep, but this time on a bed. When I awoke, I got out of bed to make a collect phone call. I had barely arrived at the phone station when the correctional officer barked, "Bryant, lockdown." I had forgotten to make my bed. I hadn't seen the outside of a cell for more than twenty seconds. Placed on two-day lockdown. Next, transferred to a regular housing unit. I was still on lockdown status, but was being transferred to a cell where another inmate was also on lockdown. "Bryant, cell 28, top bunk," the officer ordered. I walked up a flight of stairs and waited by the cell. The officer opened the cell from his station below and the inmate inside quickly jumped to his feet. He had been crouching next to the toilet.

"Oh man, I thought you were the officer," he said. "I was just smoking. Do you smoke?" I was caught off guard, but said yes. He proceeded to show me how to hold the hand-rolled cigarette by the air intake vent and slowly exhale so that the vent would suck in all of the excess smoke. My cellmate's name was Richard. He was a veteran of the United States Marine Corps and had spent a large portion of his adult life incarcerated. While living on the streets, I had encountered many veterans who were homeless and addicted to drugs. They only served to perpetuate my cynical beliefs about society. Why had all of these veterans been abandoned by the country they had served? Why were they suffering silently alongside me on the streets?

Richard had turned himself in for a parole violation; he was waiting to be transferred to a substance abuse treatment program. He was experiencing heroin withdrawals and was clearly miserable. To combat the withdrawal symptoms, he couldn't eat anything but sweets, but was constantly puking regardless. The contrast between us was obvious: he couldn't fall asleep while I wanted to sleep all day and night. Meth addicts are always behind on sleep.

Richard and I would play cards all night, work out, and take turns pacing the small space within our cell to keep busy. Richard began selling cigarettes in exchange for snacks, paper, and books. We started a routine of smoking one cigarette each hour immediately after the guard had completed his hourly round of checking in each cell. During one of these hours, we became impatient and decided to have a second cigarette, a choice that was risking discover. When the officer walked by our cell, he paused, turned around, and opened our cell.

"It smells like cigarettes, gentlemen. You been smoking?" he asked. We insisted that we had no idea what he was talking about, which prompted a search of our cell. After a thorough search, the officer found nothing. I was filled with a sense of criminal triumph. He allowed us back into our cell and after putting our cell back in order, we both laid down. Richard fell asleep quickly while I lay awake looking out the cell window.

Suddenly, at least fifteen transport officers, those responsible for moving inmates throughout the jail and responding to emergencies, stood outside of our cellblock waiting for another officer to open the door.

"Richard, cops at the door. Wake up," I whispered. By the time Richard had fully woken up, the officers were running up the stairs and immediately opened our cell door.

We were pulled roughly out of the cell and separated. I was taken into the recreation yard to be questioned. The officers were pressuring me to tell them where the cigarettes were hidden, interrogating me with threats and attempting to coerce the information out of me. I responded by telling them I had been asleep and that I don't even smoke. This only aggravated them more. They began threatening me with felony contraband charges, telling me I would be sent to prison if I didn't cooperate. They were attempting to frighten me since it was my first time in jail, but I knew this wouldn't happen. Besides, I was too entrenched in the criminal code; I held my ground.

Richard had decided he would not budge either and a closer examination of our cell still turned up nothing. The officers decided a full body cavity search was in order. We were taken to the showers, which were in full view of all the cells equipped with doors only meant to cover the midsection of a body. All of the inmates in our section had been locked down and were watching attentively. We were stripped searched in full view of the whole cellblock, the doors to the showers left intentionally open.

"Bend over, spread your cheeks, cough," the officer said. By this point I had become indifferent to the situation. Like countless times before, my psyche retreated to the recesses of my mind for protection, to escape the current circumstance.

Still no tobacco was found, but I had begun to develop resentment towards the officers. Richard finally handed over the tobacco to one of the guards and it is still a mystery to me as to where he might have been keeping it.

I was given a disciplinary infraction and locked down for an additional period of time, but ultimately it didn't matter. I was released the following day. My charges had not yet been filed and the jail could only hold me for 72 business hours. While I had been arrested on the weekend, that timeframe was up and they could no longer hold me. My first time in jail was definitely memorable.

DESPAIR

While my first time in jail may have been memorable, I was largely unaffected by it. Upon release, I went directly back to the house on the north side, undeterred by the experience of incarceration. I immediately begin using drugs and looking to find more.

I went with another guy who was at the house to a hotel called the Inn Town Suites in order to obtain more methamphetamine. Upon arriving at the hotel, we were greeted by an unfamiliar woman who put me on edge. She had long fingernails, long dark hair that fell to either side of her face, and gave an impression that could only be described as creepy. When we walked into her room, I noticed a young boy sitting on the bed who couldn't have been more than twelve years old. This was her son. I hated it when there were children around drug deals. Whenever children were around, I found it difficult to look them in the face; I knew it was wrong to use drugs and wrong to engage it criminal activity around children, but I found it was all too common. I made an awkward attempt to be friendly as I intruded on his life.

"What's up?" I asked. He said nothing. He seemed to shrink inward as he turned his eyes away in a timid gesture. A few days later I learned his mother actually prostituted him for money and drugs. I have never forgotten the look on that boy's face. Every time I reflect on this encounter, I am truly sad what this young child has gone through and how it will affect the rest of his life.

I went back to the house on the north side and proceeded to get high, once more escaping my reality. I stayed at the house for several more weeks, but some of the tenants became uneasy as traffic within the house increased. It was time to move out. Linda and I both moved to a house owned by a lady named Cindy. Although the house had recently been raided for a methamphetamine laboratory and Cindy's husband had been sent to prison, the house had turned into something of a biker clubhouse. Despite her marital status, Cindy and I began having an intimate relationship and I moved into her room. It seemed like a different life when I had held the belief that being intimate with another's man wife was wrong, but I had thrown away all of my core values in the wake on my addiction. I was seemingly unbothered by participating in the destruction of a family.

I was consuming more meth at this house than I had anywhere else. I would stay up for four or five days at a time experiencing severe states of delirium. This house seemed to drain what little was left of my spirits;

I felt like I was losing my mind, like I was empty inside, like my life was meaningless. I was experiencing an ultimate state of despair. It was during this period I first heard Eric Clapton's song, Tears in Heaven. The words resonated within me, serving only to deepen my depression as I was reminded of my father and another world I had once known in what seemed to be the distant past.

One afternoon, I headed to a gas station in Cindy's car to buy some cigarettes. I was extremely flustered because of an argument that had broken out at the house and I needed to get away from the fighting. My knuckles were white from gripping the wheel and I was delirious from lack of sleep. Something appeared in the corner of my eye and it took me a moment to realize I had run a stop sign. I swerved hard to the right with barely enough time to register that a motorcycle was swerving hard to the left, narrowly missing the car. The car skidded to a halt and the motorcycle hit the curb, dumping the driver and his young passenger off. People immediately came running from the nearby houses to see what had happened. One man started yelling at me and getting in my face. I was already angry and likely would have punched him had I not been completely caught off guard. The motorcycle driver blindsided me with a fist to the jaw, nearly knocking me down. I was furious and faced the man fully intending to retaliate. When he saw he had not hurt me, he bolted. By this point my blood was boiling and I began walking after him.

"Where are you going?" one bystander asked incredulously.

"I'm walking around the block," I replied.

"You can't leave," he began to argue, but I continued walking and ignored his protests. What transpired was like a scene from a movie: approximately twenty bystanders followed me. It was as if the mob was in slow pursuit of me! They were yelling and becoming increasingly agitated, assuming I was attempting to flee the scene. As I rounded the block by Cindy's house, police cars came screeching around the corner and I was taken down like a high profile fugitive.

I was sent to jail for failure to appear in court. A few days locked up and then I was released. It was hardly memorable. I returned to Cindy's house without hesitation.

On the evening of my return, there was a commotion at the front door around four in the morning. It turned out to be some of the men who still lived at the house on the north side. They were looking to score some drugs and were acting rather strange, but it wasn't until later that I learned of their grim situation. When the story surfaced, it turned out that one of the men's sister had overdosed on Oxycontin. The group had left her dying in an effort to obtain some meth to revive her. She died of an Oxycontin overdose. Although foul play was suspected, a substandard police investigation yielded no results, reinforcing my lack of faith in the system. While the truth still remains unclear to me, I can comfortably attest that addiction is a cold and heartless thing.

When Cindy and I discontinued our relationship, I moved into Linda's room. We began an intimate relationship that would prove to last much longer. As conflict at the house continued, we decided to try our luck at living in motels.

One of the final, but perhaps most significant memories I have while residing at this house occurred during Halloween. The memory remains so clear because it reflects the complete level of isolation I felt at the time. As usual, those at the house, including myself, were getting high while little children could be seen through the windows. They were running around the neighborhood in their costumes, laughing, playing, and existing in a world I no longer knew. Not one child came to the door in search of candy that night. It truly felt like we were invisible, disconnected from the world. The neighbors had such a negative view of the house that no visitors ever came. I assumed the previous raid had garnered a great deal of negative attention, but I was still simply astounded. This house was devoid of anything positive; this house was despair.

MOTELS

Linda and I got a room at the Allstar, a motel located on North Temple Street. Those involved in drugs and prostitution frequented this motel, an epicenter of criminal activity. We soon became enmeshed in the motel culture, a population of people living on the streets and in motels. The additional network allowed Linda and me to sell even more drugs, though we rarely made any money given our habits cost us hundreds of dollars a day.

It was at this dirty, rundown motel that I first used methamphetamine intravenously. The majority of people I associated were intravenous meth and heroin users, but I had stuck to smoking meth. When a few people, residents from the house on the north side, were visiting my motel room, I decided to try getting high via syringe. My fixation with smoke, with the visibility, the inhalation and exhalation had curbed my desire to try this method of delivery, but I was ready and willing to expand my experience. We prepared the apparatus and put the same amount of drug in each syringe. This would prove nearly fatal. I had consumed hundreds of dollars worth of drugs daily for years, but my body was not accustomed to intravenous use. My body was not ready for the injection, the breaking of skin, the rapid distribution of meth through my bloodstream. I had no business using the same amount of drug as those I was using with. Many of these people had been using syringes for twenty or so years.

As soon as the drug entered my bloodstream, my body started

shutting down. Cold sweats, body shaking, mind fading in and out of consciousness, all accompanied by an incredibly powerful draining of energy from my body. I could hear voices vaguely in the background. "What's happening?" "Lay him down, he will be okay." This was the same group of people that had failed to get emergency medical support for the woman who died of Oxycontin overdose. Slowly there voices began to fade to whispers, dreamlike utterances of apprehension, and I wondered if this would be my final memory. I awoke some time later in the bed at the Allstar, those still in the room busy getting high.

My body felt weak, my mind shaken. But I was undeterred. Having just overdosed and nearly died, the logical thing would have been to consider my substance abuse and use the experience as a turning point. Addiction is a powerful thing—I was getting high later that day.

I soon discovered that police officers were daily visitors of cockroach-infested motels such as the Allstar. Most residents kept an eye out for police to warn each other. We lived by the code of the streets: it was us against them. We got no warning when a Salt Lake City SWAT team stormed our room. They were looking for a man who had spent the last few nights in our room. When they learned he wasn't there, they eventually left and my day continued as if nothing had happened. I was becoming alarmingly accustomed to the presence of law enforcement and the chaos that attracted them. My disregard was evident in my increasingly callous and disrespectful comments made towards them. It was during our stay at the Allstar that Linda and I experienced the beginning of our domestic problems. Just like the meth had gotten under my skin, the pressure of maintaining a relationship and a drug habit was becoming more and more burdensome. Several days behind on rent and under pressure from motel management to pay or vacate, Linda prompted me to get some money. With no scams in the works, an argument ensued.

"Punk," she spat at me. I was furious. A string of derogatory terms came spilling from her lips, the ultimate disrespect in the criminal world. No one had ever talked to me like that. I left immediately. My time with gangs in the past had taught me to never allow anyone to disrespect me. I traveled to my mother's house even though I knew I wouldn't be able to stay long without access to drugs. After asking my mother for some money, I found myself in another argument. This scenario was becoming all too familiar. It would appear the domestic problems with my mother began this day as well.

I went directly back to the Allstar in hopes of getting high, the argument from earlier lost in the haze of addiction. When I arrived, several men were with Linda and she had an abundance of drugs. While this was peculiar, I initially thought nothing of it. We used all of the drugs by morning and were informed by management we were being kicked out for non-payment. Angry, delirious, coming down from the high, I proceeded to get into a verbal argument with the motel employee. Eighty-sixed. I was permanently kicked out from the hotel property.

Linda and I moved onto the Zion's motel. It was a decrepit building filled with cockroaches and residents involved in drugs and prostitution. A familiar crowd. Most of the doors couldn't close properly, the frames ruined from past drug raids. We soon discovered the majority of the rooms had been used as temporary meth laboratories, the walls left covered with a yellow film. We cleaned the walls with bleach to remove the noxious chemicals and disposed of the crack and meth pipes that would turn up hidden in the corners of the room.

We encountered many of the same people that had resided at the Allstar and began selling drugs and getting high with the prostitutes, pimps, and lowlifes of every type. We became friends with another couple that we could identify with. At the core they were good people, thoughtful and caring, but they had became trapped in the horrible world of drugs. The woman was a prostitute and while her boyfriend didn't approve, his addiction was compelling and he would leave the room during her business with clientele. Between her prostitution and his illegal endeavors, they barely made enough to maintain their drug habit and pay for rent. They were trapped in a self-perpetuating cycle of sadness and despair. When it came down to drugs versus rent, drugs always ran out, the trap of their addictions holding them in vice grips.

One day, we switched rooms with this couple and Linda and I found ourselves upgraded to a kitchenette. Apart from the usual amenities, we now had more room for cockroaches and needles. We were getting ready to make steak and spaghetti when we realized we had left our only pan back in the other room. I grabbed the garbage can to take outside, needing a legitimate objective due to the frequent police presence, and headed to their room. I was knocking on the door while calling them on my cell phone when ten detectives with badges around their necks came running around the corner with guns drawn.

"Get your hands up!" several yelled in unison.

I replied with my usual attitude. "I'm not dropping my phone. You're tripping. Why do you have a gun pointed at me?" The police officers rushed forward, one hitting me with his forearm and slamming my face into the brick building. With a bruising face and growing headache, I was handcuffed and questioned. Wondering what I was doing at the room, I explained to the officers I was just getting a pan I had left there the night before. I told them I was planning on cooking spaghetti and steak in my room.

An officer left to question Linda and investigate my bizarre claim, but quickly returned. "He's telling the truth. He has a steak freshly cooked and ready to eat," the officer said. The handcuffs were removed and the officer apologized for the physical assault, but he warned me to always follow police officer direction.

Later that week, Linda and I held round two of the argument we had begun at the Allstar motel. We needed money for rent and once again I was a punk. My blood quickly reached the boiling point. I was standing next to her while she was laying on the bed, our yells ricocheting back and forth off of each other. As our argument began to escalate, she released an up-kick that hit me directly in the jaw. I reacted faster than I could think; I struck back. I took a step back, shocked at myself, before leaving to walk down State Street.

I was extremely troubled by what had just occurred. I did not believe in hitting a woman nor had I ever done so in the past. I felt a significant degree of shame for what had transpired. I eventually returned apologetic and we quickly made up. I was reminded of the domestic violence situations I had heard about: the man hits the woman, the man comes back apologetic, the man and woman make up, and the cycle continues. Soon after this, we were eighty-sixed from the Zion's motel due to our inability to pay rent as well as our numerous encounters with law enforcement. We moved to a motel in Rose Park, the same neighborhood as Cindy's house. The Salt City Inn was equipped with all the features we were used to: cockroaches, dirty walls, used syringes, and prostitution. But this time there was something new: criminally involved staff members. We started using methamphetamine with the staff members who were involved in prostitution rings and meth manufacturing. Police officers didn't seem to frequent this motel as often as they had at others despite there being substantially more criminal activity at the Salt City Inn. The reason for this could have been the more organized operations or police corruption keeping things quiet. I would suggest the latter to be true. Kristi, Linda's sixteen-year-old daughter, was eventually allowed to move in with us. I was not happy about the arrangement. Not only was Kristi closer to my age than Linda, but also I didn't believe it was appropriate to have a child present in our chaotic lives and I didn't possess the ability to adjust. It was simply not possible for me to provide a safe place to stay and supply all the needs of a child nor did I have any desire to. Only days after Kristi began living with us, we were eighty-sixed from the Salt City Inn for the typical reasons: failure to pay and verbal arguments with management.

We all moved to Sandy City to live in the basement of a house owned by a man named Kurt. Since he was a meth addict, we paid the first month's rent with drugs. We had been there for maybe a few days when an acquaintance, Ted, came over. We went to the closest gas station to buy some cigarettes and milk when he informed me of a serious accusation. Kristi had told Ted that Kurt had offered her drugs and made sexual advances. I was thrown into an absolute rage. The next thirty minutes were spent as if I was a third party viewing my actions.

I called Linda's brother and ordered him to pick up Kristi in case the situation at the house became volatile. I began packing all of our belongings while I waited for Linda to get out of the shower. When she finished, I had already packed and loaded most of our belongings in Ted's truck and Linda's brother had picked up Kristi. Linda was thoroughly confused. I briefly explained the situation to her and started taking the final boxes out to the car.

Kurt confronted me outside. "What's going on?" he asked. "You know what you've done and the best thing you can do is lock yourself in your room until we leave," I threatened. He continued to act naïve to the situation while wearing a taunting smirk on his face. I gave him another warning, but he stood in front of me smiling, almost as if he was proud of himself. I attacked him. We ended up on the neighbor's porch, Kurt falling on the ground and me kicking him repeatedly. It was an effort to stop myself, but I managed to get back inside to house to collect the last of our belongings and leave. I was met by the Sandy Police Department on my way out the door. When all was said and done, I received an assault charge. Kurt was allowed to leave the scene without any charges. With only thirty-two dollars left, we stayed at a motel in Midvale called the Copperview, another dive full of prostitution and drugs. It took several hours for the adrenaline to wear off and for me to realize I was in need of medical attention. My foot had been broken in the assault. It was the middle of the night, but I began the two-mile journey down State Street to the nearest hospital. Perhaps three-quarters of a mile down the street, I knew there was no way I would be able to make it. With nowhere else to go, I stopped at a 24-hour adult store to call an ambulance! I spent the next several hours in the hospital getting X-rays, receiving medical care, and avoiding questions about how my foot had been broken.

I returned to the Copperview early in the morning with a cast as my new footwear. We had recently acquired a dog, half pit bull, half Rottweiler, and named him Sampson. When I took him outside so he could relieve himself, the manager saw me. As this motel did not allow dogs, we engaged in a verbal argument before the Midvale Police Department finally escorted me off of the property. Eighty-sixed from yet another motel.

We moved down the street and began settling in at a Motel Six. I had neither slept nor used drugs in the last twenty-four hours and I was exhausted. Lying on the bed, I began to doze off when Linda started an all too familiar battle. She insisted I go and fill the prescription of pain medication that I had received at the hospital so we could sell the pills and get some money for rent. I pleaded to sleep for just a few hours, but she was relentless. I exploded.

I had just moved us out of the house in Sandy to defend her daughter, had received additional criminal charges in the process, and had to go the hospital all within a twenty-four hour period and I was fed up. I jumped off the bed and began throwing all of her belongings onto the sidewalk. Plastic storage boxes were breaking and spilling their contents everywhere, but I was oblivious. She was screaming at me as I ordered her to get out of my room. The Midvale Police Department was called and rounded the corner in their patrol car right as I threw a battery through the motel window.

I was tackled, handcuffed, and scolded by the officers for having contact with me just hours earlier on top of the incident with Sandy police the night before. I was completely out of control. Motel Six management informed me I could not stay at any of their facilities anywhere in the country. I was read my rights and taken to jail.

DETOX

I went through the usual booking process: strip search, holding cell, quarantine, and finally being transferred to a regular cellblock several days later. I had been asleep for at least three days when the officer on duty yelled into the intercom, "Bryant, you have video court. Get ready." I told him I was tired and would not be going, but he coerced me into attending! I plead guilty via teleconference with no attorney present and was sentenced to forty days in jail. I returned to my cell and slept through the worst of the withdrawal symptoms, namely the nausea and complete lack of energy.

When I became coherent again, I got out of bed and started walking around the cellblock, talking with people and even working out. Every day seemed to last forever. I would walk between seven and ten miles a day in very small circles, but I was beginning to feel physically healthy again. I even began to think that upon my release I would stay clean and resolve the remainder of my court cases. I had never considered this as an option before, but feeling good both physically and mentally seemed to make it a possibility.

At one point, I met an old acquaintance, a man that had been involved in manufacturing methamphetamine at the Wayfares Inn. He was being charged with purchasing blue iodine in amounts that exceed federal law. This was an eye opener for me: he was part of the same circle of people that had purchased blue iodine at the Ball and Feed agricultural store alongside me. We chatted a while, small talk and such, but when he found out I was out of commissary and would have to wait until morning for more money to be placed on my account, he offered to give me a "two for one." He would loan me a snack food then and receive two in return at a later date. Loan sharking in its purest form!

When morning came and I received my commissary, it was time to pay him back. I stuffed the two candy bars in my pants, as it was against jail rules to trade or pass commissary, and made my way to his cell. His bunk was empty. When I asked his cellmate what had happened, I learned that federal marshals had picked him up in the middle of the night to transfer him to a federal holding facility. I later found out that he had been sentenced to a significant amount of time in federal prison for his blue iodine purchases. This could easily have been me.

EIGHTY-SIXED

I was released from jail after thirty-five days feeling stronger physically and mentally than I had in years. I was sober. I was clean. My mind was clear from the fog of intoxication and my body felt healthy and strong. This meant nothing to me.

I had absolutely no intention of staying sober; all I could think about was getting high. The first thing I did upon release was to find out where Linda was. I was back with her before the end of the night. She was living with another woman who had two sons. Nothing had changed. They were getting high all day and night and once again children were caught in the crossfire. Within twenty-four hours of getting out of jail, I was right back in the middle of this toxic circle of people, using drugs and committing crimes.

Linda and I moved out and went to the Gateway Inn on North Temple Street, an epicenter of drugs and prostitution. It was during our stay here that we met Franky. He reminded me of a weasel with his greasy hair in a curly mullet and a smarmy grin on his face. I couldn't stand him. I immediately had conflict with him, as he was trying to sell heroin out of my room and I would have no part in it. I didn't want to go back to jail and was making every effort to rid my room of drug activity. Except, of course, my own. I kicked him out of my room and threatened him with physical harm if he ever jeopardized my situation again.

One morning, a man who was staying in our room received a phone call on his cell phone. He looked around suspiciously before stepping outside the door. I got up to investigate. When I opened the door, he was standing there looking at a display of heroin balloons in Franky's hand. I was furious. I threw Franky into the second floor railing of the motel.

"Do you know who I am?" he yelled, challenging me. My thoughts went blank. I picked him up and hung him over the balcony. Time seemed to stop before I pulled him back over the balcony and set him on the ground. "It doesn't matter who you are because it could have been all over," I replied. I was absolutely shocked with myself. I could have easily dropped him by accident and caused him serious injury. What I found most troubling was that the streets were turning me cold. Over the years, feelings of compassion and morality had slowly ebbed out of me. This situation demonstrated how stale my soul was becoming.

I began stealing and utilizing other scams again in order to feed my drug habit. It was at this same time that I began noticing some oddities, some inconsistencies in my relationship with Linda. I would often leave for several hours at a time in pursuit of drugs and return to find Linda with a supply of drugs. She never had any money when I left, but there were often men present when I returned. I became very suspicious of her, but I was also having a hard time interpreting reality from intoxicated fiction. I was usually sleep deprived, high on drugs, and it was beginning to take a significant toll on my mental health. Linda would play on this whenever I questioned her, claiming I was simply being paranoid because of the drugs. I didn't know what to believe.

We ran into problems paying rent at the Gateway Inn. When this would happen, I typically would venture to my mother's house and make some pathetic attempt to coerce her into giving me money. One afternoon, I went to my mother's house with this very purpose in mind, but ended up getting into a serious verbal argument with her. I subsequently punched a hole in her wall. She called the police on me, but I managed to escape. I was becoming a monster. I was bringing chaos to my mother's life causing her to fear my presence.

Linda and I were ultimately kicked out of the Gateway Inn for our outstanding debt. We moved on to one of the worst motels in the city:

the Dream Inn, also located on North Temple Street. The Dream Inn was incredibly dilapidated, the rooms didn't even have functional doors, and the tenants were less than desirable, similar to its Zion's Motel counterpart. The management had a reputation for being involved with prostitution and trading sexual favors for overdue rent. Our very first day there, the man who ran the motel came wandering into our room while Linda was in the shower. I refused to believe this was an honest mistake and began pushing him out of the room, yelling and threatening him. We were escorted off the property by the Salt Lake City Police Department. Eighty sixed from yet another motel.

We found ourselves at the Colonial Village Motel. This motel was as luxurious as the rest: cockroaches, discolored walls and furniture, drug paraphernalia, and broken doorframes. Once again, the motel staff was involved in both drugs and prostitution. It was during our time here that I began to truly understand the extensive underground world of prostitution. Motorcycle gangs had control over the majority of the prostitutes. They would exploit them by taking most their profits. I soon learned that women were used to pay for almost anything: drugs, debts, rent, and most troubling of all, to satisfy corrupt police officers who were willing to look the other way and ignore criminal activity.

The nature of my lifestyle coupled with the viewpoints I held and my confrontational personality created many enemies. I was around groups of people that held white supremacist ideals, beliefs I openly and vocally did not share. I had also stolen large amounts of money and drugs from countless people. The threat of retaliation was omnipresent.

My dogs, Cassius and Oscar, lived at my mother's house. Both were boxers. While living at the Colonial Village Inn, I learned that Cassius had been poisoned and killed. I had a fairly good idea the group of people responsible, but no one in particular I could attribute it to. When I found

Cassius, he was lying in a pool of his own dark blood. I later found silica packets in the dog food bin, which was likely the cause of his death. Oscar was luckily quite picky with his food; I believe this prevented his demise. Although my dogs meant a great deal to me and losing Cassius was emotionally trying, my addiction was strong and I continued my lifestyle undeterred.

Our last day at the Colonial Village Inn, we were an hour behind on our rent. I was out in a rush trying to hustle up enough money to maintain our room. When I arrived back at the motel with the money, the lady at the front desk refused to accept my payment. She stated we had been late too many times and we needed to leave. I initiated an argument with her as usual and her response was calling the cops. I told Linda what had happened and escaped over a fence into an alley. Eighty sixed from the Colonial Village Inn.

At this point, I had been arrested and taken to jail ten times. Linda and I had been eighty-sixed from nineteen motels, primarily due to my erratic and sometimes violent behavior. I was losing control, falling faster each day.

RUSSIAN ROULLETTE

After some negotiation, the management at the Gateway Inn agreed to let us return with a few weeks worth of rent paid in advance. We were right back in the middle of the chaos. This episode at the Gateway Inn would prove to be a more spiritually, emotionally, and legally consequential experience than the last. These motels were catalysts of human suffering and each new residency seemed to take a little bit more from me.

I had been trading valuables from my mother's house to purchase drugs for so many years that I deserved to be incarcerated for that alone. I offered a guy, who happened to be a skinhead, some money to drive me to my mother's house. I needed to get some food, wash my clothes, and like so many times before, obtain some valuables to sell for drugs.

When we arrived back at the motel, I noticed that several of the items in the back of his truck belonged to me. There was no mistaking my grandfather's mandolin. I realized he must have gathered these items out of the garage while I had been inside my mother's house. I pulled the items out of his truck and confronted him in a threatening tone. I thought he would at least be somewhat embarrassed, but he proceeded to ask for the gas money I had promised him!

"You must be crazy," I spat at him. I told him he would get nothing from me and that he was lucky to be driving away unscathed. But he was no pushover. He exited his vehicle and pulled out a huge hunting knife with an eight-inch blade. This knife was designed for gutting animals and it was evident I was going to be the prey in this scenario.

"I'm not going to act like a punk just because you have a knife. You must have me confused with someone else," I taunted. He began stalking towards me when Linda yelled from the balcony and demanded that he stop. She was well connected and respected within the criminal circles and her command seemed to break his trance. I likely owe my well being to Linda on this occasion. This man and I had managed to lock ourselves in a stalemate, as neither was able to back down due to pride and the unspoken code of the streets.

The continual hints of prostitution within my interpersonal relationship caused me a considerable amount of anxiety. I could feel that things were going on that I was not privy to and it was driving me mad. I could often find strange text messages on our phone, which I typically noticed while Linda was in the shower. When one such text message came, I responded with very harsh words. The guy who sent the message was a member of a Salt Lake City based motorcycle gang, The Barons. His response was filled with sexually explicit implications regarding Linda. Not only did this heighten my awareness of the status of my relationship, but also his words represented an ultimate disrespect towards me. The proverbial ball was in my court as far as my response and I always seemed to go overboard.

I didn't have a ride to get to this man's residence, so I coerced my mother into transporting me to his house by telling some fictitious story regarding my need for a ride. I fully intended to fight him, but he wasn't home when I arrived. I settled for the next best thing: I broke all of the windows on the façade of his house, all while my mother watched from the car. She was furious and also scared. I had just brought her along for a criminal retaliation. It appeared that I had lost all judgment. My mind, morals, and spirit had been compromised by circumstances I had created. It seemed there was nothing left that I wasn't capable of doing.

LOST

...How had I come to this place? How did this happen? Was I that lost, that confused? Was it the years of stealing, the years of lying, the complete disregard for others, for myself? I had never been so lost and confused. A man had offered to give me money and drugs to perform sexual acts on me. I had allowed him. How could I have allowed him? I had to have the drugs. I needed the drugs. Anything to get the drugs, I needed the drugs, it didn't matter what I had to do, I needed the drugs, I didn't want him to do it, I had to hide, I had to hide in the back of my mind, become indifferent, but I had to do it, I needed the drugs...

What had I become?

I entered back into the night, a pocket full of money and drugs weighing me down, reminding me of what had just occurred. I began running, chasing the night, running faster, lungs aching, trying to escape what had just transpired. There were cars lining the streets that night, watching me, delusions catching up with me, all of the cars staring at me...shaming me. The confusion and anger that had plagued me for so many years of substance abuse were only compounded by the shame and guilt of this event. My substance abuse, my criminal activity, my fatalistic view of life ultimately increased because of the depths of addiction I had sunken to. I quickly discovered that I was not alone. There were many men, young and old, that had fallen victim to this dark and all too often unspeakable aspect of addition. Already silenced by their substance abuse, these men were succumbing to selling themselves to support the very monster that forced them into that position in the first place: addiction. Women prostituted themselves for drugs all the time; it was normal, commonplace. But this, men doing the same, it was silenced, shameful, and unspeakable. I still felt alone.

My behavior became increasingly erratic and even more aggressive, as if to prove to myself and everyone else that I was mean, tough, someone to be reckoned with. And I was. I was dangerous, unpredictable, criminal. I was tough. But I was becoming a monster, the same monster I had fallen victim to, a monster shaped and groomed by addiction.

As times continued to be desperate, I attempted to get money from my mother. Getting to her was often an obstacle, though. One day, I promised a man who had been hanging around our motel room some money if he would give Linda and me a ride to my mother's house. Jim agreed to the terms and drove us over to my mother's house.

The conversation with my mother was typical and had escalated to angry words when Linda called me. I had been inside for such a long time that Jim had left and taken Linda with him. She had called me from a nearby gas station, informed me they were trying to take her somewhere, and told me to hurry up and come get her.

I placed my dog, Oscar, on a leash and demanded a ride from my mother. Sensing the urgency in my voice, she acquiesced. I arrived at the gas station and jumped out of the car, yelling at Jim with my dog in hand. Jim looked worried and made a comment to the effect that I was using my dog because I couldn't face him alone. I lost my cool.

I tied Oscar to a pole, knocked Jim to the ground, and took turns kicking him in the side and kicking dents into his car. My mother drove away, scared and furious. Even Linda, who was used to my erratic behavior, stood frozen in disbelief. I was acting in a way that was beyond even her frame of reference. To anyone observing, it was clearly apparent that I had lost touch with reality and was an imminent danger to others and myself. Jim drove away as soon as he was able to stand while Linda and I waited for a cab to take us back to the Gateway Inn. I had a feeling that Jim would arrive at our room before we did. I was right. Once back at the hotel, our door had been kicked in and all of our valuables taken. The relative calm I had managed to achieve vanished. I was on a hunt to find this man.

I found him perhaps a week later. He was walking along North Temple Street early in the morning, bags under his eyes and that strung out look that I was too familiar with. It was clear he had been awake for several days. I snuck up behind him and shocked him when I made my presence known. I meant violence and he could tell. I pressured him about the whereabouts of our belongings until he submitted. When I walked away from him, he was lying in the middle of the street, bruised, bloody, and in danger of being run over by a car. I didn't even care. I quickly retrieved all of our belongings without a thought for the violence required to do so.

My domestic issues with Linda continued to get worse, becoming a continuous stream of arguments over drugs and money. I was finally fed up with it and called my mother for a ride, assuring her I wanted to leave for good and would meet her at Beto's fast food Mexican restaurant across the street from the Gateway Inn. She agreed to pick me up on the condition that I promised not to return to Linda. I didn't want to end up in jail while squabbling with Linda, but she had other plans.

As I was walking out the door, I was hit from behind and my head exploded with pain. Linda had hit me with frying pan! Unlike the comedy of cartoons, this was extremely painful! I got in her face and began yelling at her when she grabbed a nearby baseball bat and hit me on the arm with it. This threw me into a fury. I was almost sure my arm was broken, but I proceed to lift up the television and throw it across the room. I knew the police must be on their way and I wanted out.

Again I tried leaving the motel room, but Linda grabbed at me, kicking, scratching, and begging me not to leave. This relationship had become enmeshed with toxicity. The drugs were driving us both crazy and our lives were falling apart.

I finally made it to Beto's and had just managed to jump in my mother's car when a multitude of police officers swarmed the motel room across the street. As we drove away, the rearview mirror was flooded with flashing red and blue lights. My mother pulled over as an officer shouted into his megaphone, "Driver, passenger, put your hands out of the vehicle where I can see them." The thoughts came flooding back to me: How had I come to this place? What had I become? Had I really dragged mother into a situation where we were being extracted from the car at police gunpoint? How had I managed to sink this low?

Linda and I were ordered to remain apart for forty-eight hours by the police, as required by law. I stayed at my mother's house, but I couldn't keep my promise to her. With withdrawals setting in, I went immediately back to the motel after the appropriate time had passed to get more drugs. When I arrived, men were in the room and Linda had both money and drugs.

Everything was beginning to make sense. It was obvious what had transpired while I was gone, what had been happening all along, but I didn't want to consciously acknowledge it. Denying it made if easier for me to ignore it, to overlook the obvious.

PILOT LIGHT

I have been awake for five days now.

I am walking the streets of Salt Lake City. Purposefully. Gotta get some money. My thoughts are scattered, loose, erratic, but I know I must find a way to get some money. I am walking down North Temple Street when I see the sun peaking over the horizon. To my right, a transient man pushing his grocery cart. To my left, in the plasma center parking lot, a man slumped over and hanging out of a car. Is he dead? A closer look...it appears he has been shot. The lady in the wheelchair. Does she see him? No, she's just waiting for the center to open to give her plasma donation. How ironic. There's enough blood on the ground to save several lives. The car looks out of place, like it was pulled to a quick halt, like it doesn't belong there. His feet are still in the seat, but his upper body is hanging out of the car. It's laughable, surreal. It's tangible and grizzly. I look at the only 25-cent payphone left in Salt Lake City that I know of and think for a second that I should call, but I don't want to deal with that, with the police report. I am in a hurry. I have to catch a train across town if I'm to get this money. Gotta get some money.

Gotta get high...

My emotions at this time were like the pilot light in a furnace. I had become hard and cold on the outside, everything on the inside was dark and possibly colder...except for a small pilot light of life, a light threatened by extinction. I knew that if I continued my substance use for much longer, the pilot light would be extinguished. Never to be lit again. One of my final memories from the Gateway Inn centers on a drug deal that had gone bad. A man named Brandon had been hanging around our room all day selling crack and using heroin. He was rather large and intimidating, but I despised him. I was disgusted as I listened to him talk his girlfriend into prostitution. She had been selling herself to support their habit, but she told him she didn't want to anymore. She was just one of many young women caught in this dilemma of addiction. I was appalled while he proceeded to talk her into meeting a customer anyway. After she left, Brandon turned to me and asked if I wanted to make ten dollars. He needed me to deliver twenty crack rocks at twenty dollars a piece to a lady across the street at Beto's. This crime was enough to cause imprisonment for ten years, but I didn't care. As much as I despised him, I needed the money. I grabbed my dog, Sampson, headed across the street and sold the drugs before meeting him on the other side of Beto's.

He attempted giving me five dollars and a pack of cigarettes for my troubles, but I wasn't having it. I began demanding the money, yelling and threatening him. He refused. It was one in the morning and a crowd of drug addicts gathered around the picnic tables outside of Beto's. It was a common spot for our kind to hang out. I noticed among the crowd an acquaintance that went by the street name, Nuccus. I handed him my dog and told him to meet me back at my room, as he had stayed with us on occasion. Then I went after Brandon.

The way I had learned to be respected was by being erratic, Unpredictable, and never allowing people to take advantage of me. I was confused when Brandon ran into Beto's, but I pursued him anyway. Once inside the restaurant, he pleaded with me to back down—but to no avail. I continued my pursuit of him even when he ran behind the counter to where the cooks were. I followed him behind the counters and assaulted him. He flew into the cooks and dishes and food scattered everywhere. I had seemingly lost my mind.

I met Nuccus back at my motel room and watched as an ambulance, fire truck, and ten police cars arrived and circled around Beto's. I waited nervously, knowing at any moment police officers would come knocking at my door. They never came. The code of the streets prevented Brandon from telling the police who I was or where I was staying. It was at this moment that I realized the street code was lacking in both substance and validity. It had protected me and hidden my unjust actions. What I had done was not only wrong, but I was a dangerous person—being protected by an unspoken code of darkness.

PREDATOR

Linda and I were eighty-sixed from the Gateway Inn due to the sheer amount of domestic issues and police contact we experienced while staying there. Owing hundreds of dollars with no ability to pay also contributed to our dismissal. We went to a nearby Motel Six on North Temple Street, but had to have someone else put the room in their name given my problem at the other location.

That first evening, I walked onto the balcony and saw a slim, average-looking guy leaning up against the railing while smoking a cigarette. He introduced himself as Will and told me he had some methamphetamine. He invited Linda and I to come to his room and partake of his poison. We soon discovered he sold the drug and had in his possession a large amount. When we arrived back at our room, I devised a plan to take Will's drugs, money, and merchandise by force. I called Will early the next morning to tell him I would be stopping by to purchase some of his product. I instructed Linda to pack all of our belongings so we could vacate the premises hastily. I walked to Will's room with the intention of assaulting him and taking everything from him.

I had become a predator. My prey, anyone; my goal, drugs.

When I knocked on the door, it swung open slightly on its hinges. I opened the door quietly to a room strewn with bottles of empty alcohol. The smell of sweat and beer was rancid. Will was passed out on his bed surrounded by the aftermath of a small party he must have had since I was there hours earlier. I quickly grabbed a shoebox and a black bag filled with merchandise and ran back to my room, leaving his door cracked to come back for more. When I had the chance to inspect the stolen articles, I found nearly two ounces of meth, $1500 street value, along with a scale and some other valuable paraphernalia. It was time to leave.

As Linda and I were walking down North Temple Street holding this large amount of drugs, I never felt so exposed. North Temple Street is one of the worst places to be walking with drugs. Anyone in this area is suspect due to the high concentration of criminal activity. It didn't help that I had a $20,000 warrant for my arrest due to noncompliance with court. We made our way to the closest drug dealer's house we knew, selling enough of the product to afford another motel room. We ended up at another despicable motel, the Travel Lodge, located a few miles away on North Temple Street.

END GAME

It took perhaps three days for Linda and I to use all of the drugs from the robbery; we were subsequently kicked out of the Travel Lodge. I came up with a desperate idea: Will had been passed out on his bed when I first stole from him. Perhaps I could do it again. I called him with the intent of setting up another robbery.

When I arrived back at the Travel Lodge to meet Will, he was essentially out of drugs, but gave me a small amount to hold me over until later in the day. I could only assume he knew my intentions and wanted me as far away as possible. I had become like a deadly virus. Linda and I left Will's room and began walking back towards downtown Salt Lake City.

On our way, we came across a condemned house that we decided to explore. Houses would often be condemned after being used as meth laboratories. We would frequently break into them in search of valuable chemical contraband; red phosphorus and blue iodine, chemicals used to manufacture methamphetamine, were of particular interest.

Personal items were scattered around the house, as everything is left behind due to the hazardous chemical residue. Linda began going through these piles while I broke into the house to explore. When I entered, I realized just in time that all of the floorboards had been removed. I nearly fell through the floor to the basement! I backed out of the house and told Linda we should go. A gun appeared around the corner of the house followed by a police officer's arm.

"Put your hands up!" he yelled.

It was all over and I knew it. I felt defeated, but also a sense of relief. The officer must have read this in my body language. "You're wanted, aren't you?" he asked.

"Yeah," I replied. They started searching my backpack, most likely in search of drugs, but all they found were fifteen fruit pies and a folder full of court documents. The fruit pies were from a snack food factory. We would climb on the loading docks to steal snacks when we were hungry. The court documents consisted of four different court appearance records as well as falsified community service hours I intended to submit to the necessary courts.

I was arrested and on my way to jail with no plans of freedom in the near future. The police officer searched my person as well, but did not find the drugs hidden in my bandana. During the ride to jail, I stuffed the bandana in between the officer's seat, hoping he would not find it and I would avoid any additional charges. I was successful.

When the car arrived at the jail, the large security gates welcomed me one last time. "Officer Jones, transporting one male," the officer said into the intercom. The long intake process awaited me.

Ten hours later, I was placed in a holding cell with seven other inmates. I remained in there for thirty hours before being transported to a quarantine unit. I have little recollection of what transpired in the next few days.

AWAKE

I woke up five days later: cellblock 7A, cell 28, top bunk. I couldn't sleep anymore and needed to get out of bed. I had been placed in a medium security unit and was allowed out of my cell for approximately six hours a day.

I went to court my first week in jail for my warrant, the court case from my original arrest for vehicle burglary. Although I had no lawyer present, the judge was not willing to wait any longer to sentence me; the case was already several years old. I was sentenced to six months of suspended jail time, the full amount for the crime committed. I didn't care. I had three other judges I would have to eventually appear before and I was more concerned about the possibility of being sent to prison in one of the other courts.

When I arrived back at the cellblock, the realization hit me that this would be my home for a while. Making due with what I had, I began an intense workout regimen: pushups, dips, curl ups, jumping jacks, shadow boxing. I also began reading vigorously, often reading around five hundred pages a day.

The meals were small and despite having been strung out on drugs when I first arrived, I was still losing weight. The last meal of the day was at four in the afternoon and the next meal wasn't until six in the morning. I had never experienced anything quite like that and began having trouble sleeping at night. I soon switched my sleeping routine; I stayed up all night until breakfast was served and would then fall asleep. I simply could not sleep on an empty stomach. Only after the morning meal could I finally get some rest.

I eventually appeared in front of a judge regarding an incident that had occurred at the Gateway Inn. This particular judge had a reputation for running sentences from her court consecutive with others. Knowing my sentences would likely have to be served back to back, I decided I had nothing to lose and was completely honest. I pled guilty so as not to take more of the court's time than was necessary. The judge must have respected my accountability because the six-month sentence she gave me was to be run concurrent with the other sentence. With two more judges to go, I was beginning to feel more confident about being given reasonable sentences.

As I began to settle into life in jail, I realized I was surrounded by people with nothing to lose. Many were on their way to prison while others, including myself, had been hardened by harsh lifestyles and had seemingly lost the motivation to live positive and productive lives. The stress of living in close quarters, the loss of freedom, and opposing personalities was a recipe for conflict. I witnessed many fights while staying in medium security. One of the worst resulted in an inmate leaving in a stretcher, convulsing and bleeding from the head. He was sent to the University of Utah Medical Center after having his head smashed into the cement and suffering from brain hemorrhages. Although I was no longer living on the streets, it was obvious to me that my current living situation was just as potentially dangerous.

MEMORIES

She did it. She had finally had enough. My mother had filed a restraining order against me. I knew I deserved it on some level, but I didn't see it coming. When I was called down to the officer's station one morning and met by the constable, I wasn't expecting to be served with a restraining order. But there it was, a physical reflection of the fear and distress I had caused my mother. She had experienced more than she could bear. Standing there, restraining order in hand, it hit me that I was on my own. I had been cut off.

I was disgusted with myself.

I was soon transferred to another medium security unit: 4A. Full of gang members and foul tempers, I witnessed many fights in this unit that often led to the section being locked down. I met a guy with the street name, Twin. Nobody could stand him. Barely 110 pounds, he would try and pick fights with everyone and always had his hand down his pants! He was in jail for murder and had been for quite some time, fighting his conviction. I soon found out, from discussions with other inmates, that Twin had reportedly shot a man during a drug deal and left him to die in his car in the parking lot of a plasma donation center on North Temple Street. I couldn't believe it. What was the likelihood? Could it really be? Could this be the same plasma center, the same shooting, the same body hanging limply from the driver's side of the car? This was how my life was unfolding; this synchronicity was representative of what I could expect from my life. I couldn't help but think of a phrase I learned on the streets, a phrase that captured what I was experiencing: *As the world turns.* I had surrendered my life to drugs, my ambition, my health, my dreams, my dignity. Drugs had led me to a world that had stolen a piece of my soul, that had made me cold, that had stripped me of my drive for life and left me with scattered images and memories of hate, mistrust, and anger. Here I was in jail, trying to piece my life back together when I meet the perpetrator of the crime I had walked away from in a plasma center parking lot because all I could think about was getting more drugs.

As the world turns.

MENTAL HEALTH

My cellmate in section 4A was extremely uninteresting. He slept all day and never spoke; passing time in this cell was arduous. When he was released unexpectedly, I found myself alone in the cell, but excited at the prospect of getting a new cellmate. I hoped to get one who was at least able to carry on a conversation, perhaps even one who enjoyed working out. When I learned my new cellmate would be coming from suicide watch, I knew my situation would soon become more interesting. Inmates placed in this section of the jail are housed alone and provided with only a tear-proof blanket in the room to prevent self-harm. This would be my first experience with mental illness of such severity.

We actually got along pretty well. We would often pass time by reminiscing about our favorite foods we enjoyed outside of jail, as if dreaming of them would assuage the desire. During one of our cell cleaning days, it became evident how mentally ill this man actually was. While cleaning, he would gather excess paper towels and save them in his drawers. Late at night, he would draw "inventions" and refer to the paper towels as his scrolls. His inventions included things like underwater trains and flying snowboards, all of which had supposed dimensions and mathematical formulas for how they would work. He would put his scrolls in envelopes and mail them to the governor and the Department of Defense. He claimed we would soon have commissary, as soon as the inventions had been purchased and money placed in his inmate account.

Sadly, he never received any money on his account, and thus we had no commissary in our cell. He decided selling his medication would be an effective way of obtaining commissary. Some inmates were willing to use any drugs available including the powerful antipsychotic medications my cellmate was using. Incarceration does not negate the compulsion of addiction. When he stopped taking his meds and started dispersing them among the other inmates, madness ensued. He didn't sleep for days, he began hearing voices, and he became extremely delusional. When he became vocally suicidal, he was eventually transported back to suicide watch.

During my entire stay in jail, I had been attempting to become a trustee in order to reap the benefits of the position. Trustees are given the responsibility of serving food to other inmates and cleaning the showers, floors, and halls of the jail. Trustees also are given extra food when it is available and are allowed out of their cells more often. I had been bugging one officer for some time to get me a job and he finally found me one. I was transferred to another medium security unit, section 2A. Upon entering my cell, I was greeted by a familiar face that I had met at the house on the north side: Jesse Cochran. As the world turns.

Jesse had been incarcerated for nearly a year and a half and was waiting to be released on an ankle monitor. It was quite a surprise to be seeing him again. The specific smell of this cell imprinted quickly in my mind: there was food in here! The lack of smells in the jail made anything foreign easily detectable. Whenever an officer would bring in outside food or return from a cigarette break, the entire cellblock would quickly be full of that scent.

Only hours after being in the new cellblock, the officer on duty called me: "Roll up, Bryant." I had been in medium security for forty days without disciplinary warnings and was being reclassified to minimum security. While I was unhappy about losing my trustee job the very day I had obtained it, I was excited to have more privileges. As a minimum security inmate, I would be allowed out of my cell for several more hours a day and would have access to more support groups.

HOPE

I was transferred back to the first unit I had been in, 7A, as it had been transformed from a medium security to a minimum security unit. I also began receiving commissary at this time. My mother's name appeared on my account receipt, which could only mean something had motivated her to put money on my account. Even though she hadn't written or visited, this instilled hope within me. I had worried that I had permanently ruined my relationship with my mother, but this appeared to be a sign that she had not yet given up on me.

I soon obtained another trustee position in this unit. Even though I was incarcerated, for the first time in a decade my life was actually improving. By eating any extra available trays and continuing my workout regimen, my physical heath improved and I gained thirty pounds in my first month as a trustee. I even thoroughly enjoyed cleaning the cellblock and participating in clothing exchanges when the inmates would trade in their dirty clothes for clean ones. The work not only made the time pass, but also seemed to provide some meaning to my life, something I hadn't experienced for a long time. Between working, playing handball, working out, and reading, I was fairly content in jail. It was truly a step up from the streets: a warm bed, regular food, the chance to sleep. I was feeling good physically and beginning to think more clearly.

On one occasion, something troubling happened. Our cell doors had opened, we had been asked to stand in line, and we were waiting for the officer on duty to explain guidelines for the shift. "Hey, what the hell are you doing?" the officer suddenly yelled.

A man on the second tier was standing on the railing with a towel wrapped around his head. "I am going swimming," he said placidly. He lost his balance for a moment and almost fell. Everyone in the cellblock was frozen in anticipation.

"Someone grab him!" the officer called. Another man, still dressed in quarantine uniform, half asleep, and likely coming off of drugs, tackled the first to the ground.

The man who nearly jumped had been to court earlier in the day and sentenced to six months. He had already served one month, received commissary, and had bi-weekly visits, so most of the inmates thought his suicidal gesture was crazy. They could not conceptualize this inmate's internal despair.

The Salt Lake County Jail was a difficult place to be incarcerated. There is little to do and large portions of time are spent locked in a cell. Depression runs rampant. The skin of the inmates would often become a pale, pasty white due to the depravation of sunlight and spirits were often equally stale. I would often find myself thinking of how long it had been since I had been able to look at something as simple as a tree.

Once while playing on the handball court, a two-hundred square foot enclosure surrounded by thirty-foot walls, I saw a seagull fly by and became incredibly excited. Society's "correctional" system appears to put people that suffer from low self-esteem, trauma, and seemingly hopeless lives into an equally hopeless environment in order to induce change. This seagull seemed to represent an ultimate freedom, a freedom that incidents such as these had caused me to long for.

ASSESSED

Many inmates talked about being released early from jail by enrolling in residential substance abuse treatment programs. Apparently, if an inmate submitted a kite, a jail request form, to some woman named Jill demonstrating an interest in treatment, she would perform an assessment and possibly connect the inmate with residential treatment options. Even though I was unsure about how open I was to the idea of treatment, I knew it had to be better than my current situation.

Jill was a bright redheaded lady with an equally bright personality. Her assessment consisted of a series of questions evaluating my family history, drug use, and criminal history. She approved me for treatment funding and recommended a release to an agency called First Step House when a bed became available. I had heard good things about First Step House from other inmates, but mostly I couldn't wait for the chance to sleep in a real bed and eat quality food.

That same week I attended two court hearings, one in Sandy City and one in Taylorsville. The Sandy court sentenced me to a year in jail with the opportunity for early release to a substance abuse treatment program. The charges presented in the Taylorsville court were staggering. I had four domestic violence charges, a handful of disorderly conduct charges, and several destruction of property charges. I couldn't even recall four incidents of domestic violence; this was troubling to me. I began to understand how deserving I was of incarceration. The judge allowed me to enter a plea in abeyance. If I complied with treatment and probation, my charges would be dropped. If I failed to comply, my charges would be enhanced to a second-degree felony. In the eyes of the law, this would make me equal to someone who had been charged with aggravated assault or kidnapping.

When I arrived back at the cellblock, I decided to play some handball. Only eight people were allowed on the court at once, two teams of two played while the others waited to challenge the winner. One guy was a member of the Black Mafia Gangsters (BMG) and he insisted on playing by himself. I told him he had to find a teammate because of those waiting to play.

"I'm not playing with anyone else. You're all a bunch of bums," he retorted.

I couldn't believe it. Knowing this environment required men to show no weakness, I responded immediately. "You're crazy coming out here calling seven other guys bums."

He challenged me. "What's anyone going to do about it?" He was clearly attempting to flaunt his power. His size alone was intimidating; he was a large man at least six and a half feet tall. My adrenaline was pumping. I hated being put in this position, but I had to act.

"I may be a bum on the handball court, but I'm not a bum at fighting," I said, standing in his face. His response could have jeopardized my freedom; there was a mandatory year sentence for assault on another inmate. "Whatever, man," he said and walked away. I was truly relieved. What a ridiculous game of chicken our criminal pride had caused us to play. These ideals had become so deeply ingrained in my thoughts that I had essentially been willing to risk my life for them.

After we were locked down later that night, there was a lot of yelling in the unit. This was common after hours making jail a very hard place to get any rest. This night was different from the usual commotion somehow. There was yelling from the trustee cell next to me directed at the BMG member from my earlier confrontation. The trustees were yelling different racial slurs and threatening to give him a "rapo" tray. Trustees would intentionally pick the smallest hot tray and the smallest cold tray to give to an inmate. This was usually reserved for inmates with sexual offenses, but also happened for inmates having issues with the trustees.

The following morning, the other trustees instructed me to deliver a rapo tray to the BMG member. His cell happened to be on the top tier, the tier I was responsible for. Trustees typically act as a team and look out for each other, but I refused despite the conflict I had with this guy the day before. I went up to his cell and called him to his cuff port, the small slot in the cell door for inmates to receive food trays or be handcuffed. He looked confused.

I explained to him that I would have no part in the racist nonsense that existed within the unit and that he should wait for me to deliver his trays in the future. I told him not to accept trays from any other inmates and that he would receive a regular portion. He seemed shocked.

"Uh...good looking out," he replied.

RESILIENCY

"Bryant, roll up," yelled a voice through the cell intercom. I rolled over slowly, willing myself to wake up. It was still the middle of the night and it took me a few moments to gather myself. Realizing that I was likely being transported to First Step House, I hastily rolled up my belongings, suddenly wide awake. The thought of getting out of jail, even if it was to a substance abuse treatment facility, was extremely exciting.

When the guard finally arrived at my cell, I asked him where I was going. He informed me that I was being transported to another section of the jail. My heart sank. I was no longer happy about this transport. A new jail section meant losing my trustee job, one of the few things that made my time in jail more bearable. I asked the transport officer the reason for my transfer. He shrugged his shoulders and told me I was going to the programs unit.

We arrived at 7D, a unit located on the opposite side of the jail. Upon entering the cellblock, it became immediately clear this unit was different than most. Posters covered most of the walls, some with quotes, others with pictures. I was initially confused until I realized where I was—the Corrections Addictions Treatment Systems (CATS) program. This realization was not comforting. I was hoping a mistake had been made. If I was already in a program, I would not have the opportunity to be transferred to First Step House and would spend at least the next three months incarcerated. I was shown to a bed and fitfully tried to fall asleep. When I woke up several restless hours later, I ran into an acquaintance I had met in another section of the jail. We had been part of a workout team, as many inmates workout in groups, and I considered him a friend. "What's up, Sin?" I said with a nod. Sin was his street name.

"Hey man, you can't call me that here," he said quickly. "We don't use street names in this unit."

"Are you serious?" I asked incredulously. He began explaining the rules and expectations of the cellblock, the treatment group schedule, and other in and outs of the program. I was considering telling the corrections officer that I wanted to be taken back to the regular population, but my friend talked me into giving the program a try.

He introduced me to a workout team he had created in the cellblock, a group of approximately ten other inmates that participated. We started out by jogging several miles in the handball yard, a goal that required a few hundred laps to achieve. Working out with this team everyday helped me ease my way into this community of inmates; the increased motivation by being part of a group was another perk.

When my first Monday morning in CATS arrived, our cells were opened after breakfast one hour earlier than the rest of the jail. We started groups at eight in the morning and would continue until four in the afternoon. I was already feeling nervous about the prospect of attending All Community Meeting (ACM), the first morning meeting of the day. An unfamiliar sight greeted me when I walked into the community room: all 64 inmates of the unit were sitting in a large circle discussing the agenda and treatment issues! I was asked to introduce myself. My nervousness peaked; I hated speaking in public. I mumbled an introduction and the director of the program stood to welcome me. I knew him. He was a therapist at an outpatient program I had court-ordered to complete, but had only attended twice.

"You look much better than the last time I saw you." he remarked with a grin. As the world turns.

After ACM, we dispersed into smaller groups and participated in various activities throughout the day. We would discuss issues and work on assignments that helped us gain insight into our substance abuse and develop alternatives for the future. This became the daily schedule during my time in the CATS program.

What stood out to me the most while attending these groups was the tremendous amount of strength all of us possessed, a strength that had become overshadowed by substance abuse and criminal activity. These groups brought the strength back into the light. Pain, loss, anger, and trauma of all types were common themes among the inmates, but one trait stood out beyond all of these: resiliency. The perseverance of the human spirit, our perseverance, became evident as we shared intimate experiences with one another, experiences that often brought tears, anger, and even laughter.

Ever since my father's death, I had never had a forum for really talking about anything. I had never taken the time to share, to discuss my feelings, my worries and concerns, the intense amount of anger I had buried deep within me. I had never discussed my father's death with any meaning to it. I had never been able to do so without completely shutting down. But I had managed to find some solitude in jail, to find sobriety, to separate myself from the negative influences I had constantly surrounded myself with. For me, treatment was about the connections I made with others, people who had experienced trauma and loss just like myself. Having a forum to share some of my painful experiences was the beginning of my recovery.

PAIN

One of the hardest aspects of CATS was seeing people get kicked out. The rules were strictly enforced and inmates held each other accountable in this section. Anyone caught passing commissary, engaging in verbal confrontations, or violating rules of any kind was likely to be kicked out of the program. For many of the inmates, including myself, CATS was our last chance; failure to successfully complete the program meant a trip to the penitentiary. We were individuals who had exhausted the legal system and were beginning to be those members of society nobody wants. While in CATS, I attended a court review in Taylorsville and learned the program was highly regarded by the judges. I would be released from jail upon completion of the program and ordered to complete outpatient treatment. I had made significant improvements in my life without even leaving jail. With only the Sandy City court left to resolve, I began writing letters to the judge early to ensure a review around the time of my graduation. I was eventually informed that a court date had been set up three days after my expected graduation. I was beginning to see a very attractive light at the end of the tunnel. The end of the tunnel would be stepping out of jail into warm sunlight with the opportunity to change my life.

One night while in treatment, I began experiencing excruciating tooth pain. Like many addicts, methamphetamine had completely destroyed my teeth; it would require a great deal of dental work in the near future. One tooth had been chipped, causing my mouth to be swollen with intense pain. I hated the idea of pulling out my own tooth, but the pain was so bad I decided to take matters into my own hands.

Grabbing my flimsy jail issue toothbrush and a cup, I placed them strategically in my hand and mouth intending to dislodge the tooth with them. I hit the cup and a surge of pain traveled trough my head. It hadn't worked. I tried several more times, but only succeeded in further damaging the tooth and increasing my pain.

I dealt with the pain for three day before breaking down and finally seeing the jail dentist. The only procedures available in the jail were tooth extractions and temporary fillings. As I wandered through the jail with the transport officers picking up other inmates to see the dentist, I observed many in the same situation as my own: dental issues resulting from our drug use.

Once in the dental office, we were taken one by one, placed in the chair, given Novocain, and then our teeth were extracted. This happened in rapid succession like a production line, a practice in ultimate efficiency! I watched three people ahead of me get their teeth pulled. It quickly became apparent that Novocain didn't have the same effect on a chronic intravenous substance abuser as it would on anyone else. Those that went before me spent the length of the procedure yelling and holding white-knuckled onto the chair. I was not as unfortunate as those who went before me. The uncomfortable part for me was hearing my tooth crunch in my skull as the dentist used what appeared to be a regular pair of pliers to extract the decimated tooth.

ANXIETY

My graduation day finally arrived. I was anxious, excited, a confused paradox of emotion. I had written a speech to read in front of all the inmates in the program who would then respond, one by one, on my treatment progress and the relationships we had built. I included specific goals I planned to obtain. As my mother worked for Salt Lake Community

College, I had sent her a list of classes I wanted to attend, as I wanted to begin school in June. Although I hadn't received any response back from her, a family friend informed me she had indeed registered me and that I could move back home.

I set a goal of having an amateur boxing match within two months of my release. I would check into outpatient treatment and probation within twenty-four hours of release. Finally, I would seek gainful employment and have a job within the first month of release. Time specific goals had been stressed as an important part of success within the program. While writing my speech and reflecting back on my early life, I realized most of the goals I had actually achieved were due to having a specific plan.

I could not sleep the night before my court date. I wanted to assume my release was a sure thing, but knowing my sentence was not fully served caused me to question this. Thinking about my release and realizing the possibility of walking out of jail the next day churned my stomach. I felt simultaneously elated and scared. I had been in jail for seven and a half months. Prior to that, I had been using drugs heavily for ten years. What came next was foreign to me.

After only an hour or two of restless sleep, the morning officer yelled into my intercom, "Bryant, get ready for court." I dressed hurriedly and then my cellmate wished me well with a high five that transitioned into a half hug. The typical male greeting or goodbye. I was reminded of the pre-game prayer of some professional sports teams. I gathered my graduation certificate and began the long journey to the courthouse.

When I was finally in front of the judge, my stomach was doing flips and my anxiety was through the roof. My court appointed attorney submitted my certificate of completion along with my other support attendance forms to the judge.

"Well, it looks like you have been busy and spent your time well. What did you learn in CATS?" the judge asked.

I was not prepared with a well thought out and articulate answer. I hesitated only a moment before responding. "I learned about different types of thinking errors and I also learned how to speak in front of people when I served on the steering committee, a part of the therapeutic community that leads our group meetings." I took a deep breath before adding, "But I'm pretty nervous now."

"You are doing fine," the judge assured me. "I am going to recommend your release from jail and order that you follow through with both probation and CATS outpatient treatment." A huge smile crept across my face that I simply couldn't hide. I felt like cheering out loud!

I arrived back at the jail and was strip-searched for the last time. I was still very anxious and couldn't wait to be told to roll up. I knew it took several hours for the court order to process, but the suspense was killing me. I kept asking the guard if the order was on his computer, but the answer kept coming back no. I had all of my possessions wrapped up and ready to go, but after a few hours my mind began speculating nervously. Was there another court case or warrant I wasn't aware of? Had the paperwork failed to be completed?

"Roll up, Bryant!" the officer yelled. I sprinted to my room, grabbed my bundle, and waited for the transport officer to come for me. He finally came while I was sitting in the community meeting. As I walked away, the inmates stopped the meeting, stood up, and gave me a round of applause. It felt good.

The cellblock door closed behind me and I found myself waiting in a hallway with other inmates being transported to different places in the jail. I turned and began talking to one of the inmates when an officer barked, "Bryant, do you want to wait for the next transport to go home?"

I replied that I did not and he said, "Well, don't talk in my halls then."
I was not free yet.

I eventually made it to the release area of the jail where I was "dressed out" in a similar cell to the one I had "dressed in" nearly eight months earlier. When I opened the bag with my clothes, a stench of cigarette smoke and filth escaped. The clothes I had been wearing when I came to jail were pathetic. I realized how badly I must have smelled, the stench locked in this bag like a time capsule.

When given the chance to make a phone call, I called my mother to see if she was going to pick me up. She sounded extremely ill. I couldn't help but think the apprehension of my release must have caused her such stress that her body had responded negatively. She agreed to meet me at the Maverick gas station next to the Salt Lake County Jail.

I made my way down the release corridor, a hallways marked by painted footsteps and written directions on the wall. It was a solemn walk, silent and thoughtful.

DAYLIGHT

May 1, 2006. I walked out of the jail and into the bright sunlight. I was amazed at how beautiful the weather was. It had been so long since I had been exposed to open sunlight and it was a little overwhelming. I couldn't quite grasp my reality. I was out of jail. No one was monitoring me. I was allowed to simply enjoy the sunlight.

I was free...

I walked eagerly to the Maverick gas station, ready to buy a Pepsi and some snacks. Walking down the candy aisle made me realize the time that had elapsed during my incarceration. There were candy bars I had never seen before, variations in white chocolate or peanut butter. I was like a kid in a candy shop. Literally. I spent all of my money and waited outside, gorging myself on these new discoveries.

When my mother arrived, we greeted each other hesitantly, awkward smiles and eyes to the ground before beginning the journey home. When we pulled onto a 50-mile per hour road, I started gripping the sides of my seat with fear. It felt like we were going several hundred miles per hour; I hadn't moved this fast in a long time!

The destruction waiting for me at home blindsided me. The basement and garage were full of boxes and items strewn everywhere. In my efforts to find anything of value to fuel my addiction, I had ripped through the house and left destruction in my wake. My room was full of useless items, hundreds of cords, a myriad of dismantled electronics. I had caused this. This destruction was my fault. Meth users often dismantle objects while tweaking and collect useless materials. Here was the evidence staring me in the face.

I couldn't sleep in there. I couldn't sleep amidst the reminders of the blurry nightmare I had been living. I would have to sleep on the floor for a while. Anything to escape the reality of my past that was staring me in the face.

I threw on some clothes my mother had purchased for me to wear and went to check in with CATS outpatient treatment. The first requirement was successful completion of a urinalysis test and already I was having a difficult time producing a sample while being observed. I was not excited at the prospect of submitting samples twice a week while in treatment. I was assigned to two groups a week and would begin the following evening.

When I arrived at the probation office, I was assigned to the same probation officer I had prior to my incarceration. She had recommended jail previously and would probably be furious to find out I had been assigned to her! As the world turns. She commented on how much better I looked physically and informed me that if I attended school and submitted decent grades, I wouldn't be required to obtain full-time employment.

Next I headed to boxing. I was well on my way of establishing all of the short-term goals I had identified in my CATS graduation speech. When I arrived at the boxing gym, the coaches began making fun of how much weight I had gained, telling me I would have to fight in the heavyweight division. They commented on how good I looked and asked if I was planning on fighting anymore. The answer was a definite yet. I started training everyday, shedding pounds, sparring daily, and getting in the best shape of my life.

My zeal for life and desire to remain busy was almost frenetic. I began working on projects at home, starting with the garage. I spent an entire day emptying the garage, organizing tools, cleaning the mess, and creating a huge pile of garbage to be hauled away. Next day was the basement. By the end of the day, the pile of garbage in my driveway was large enough to require immediate attention. My mother gave me the number of a guy who hauled off people's trash as a side job and I quickly gave him a call. When he arrived to haul off the trash and saw the work I had done, he began talking to me about a job. I discussed my situation with him and he offered to let me work on the days I was out of school once I had started college.

The work was new and challenging everyday. Some days were spent demolishing the interiors of houses with sledgehammers and pry bars, while other were spent hauling off broken up cement. Working not only brought purpose to my life, but also provided me with the ability to pay for treatment costs and have some extra spending money. The flexible schedule allowed for my success in school.

My first semester in college was invigorating. Sociology, psychology, humanities, writing. All of my classes were fascinating. I had not learned anything positive for so long that I couldn't help but love it. I attempted to soak up as much information as I could. I had spent nearly the entire .com boom and computer explosion high on drugs and I was far behind my generation on technical ability. It was during this semester I first learned how to send an email and to use a thumb drive to save files.

My success in school, treatment, and boxing increased with every passing day. After much preparation, I finally received a fight in the 178-pound weight class. I was in great shape and ready for the match. I came out aggressive in the first round, breaking my opponent's ribs within a minute, but he was tough and continued to fight. At the end of the fight, he won by judge decision. The crowd went crazy with dissent, booing and yelling at the judge. I was robbed. I remembered what I hated about boxing and was determined to never let a fight go to decision again.

After the fight, a boxing coach approached me and asked if I wanted to start fighting professionally for him. Although this was my plan, I did not want to be taken advantage of. Knowing that boxers are among the most exploited of athletes, I did not want to be abused. I informed the coach I intended to fight in the Golden Gloves State Championships before turning professional. He was disappointed, but appeased.

I continued to train vigorously and approached treatment with the same determination, quickly progressing through CATS outpatient treatment. I attended AA meetings and actively participated in groups, which helped me stay grounded and focused on recovery. Many of the peers I hung out with from treatment were still engaging in risky behavior. We would go out to nightclubs, primarily for the social aspect, but by the end of the night I was the only one still sober. This wasn't working for me. I decided

I didn't want to hang out at nightclubs and I definitely didn't want to put up with drunken people.

Many of my peers ended up using drugs, often while drunk, while other ended up with DUIs and other criminal charges. I realized that in order for me to meet my treatment goals, I needed to surround myself with people conducive to my recovery. While eliminating negative influences, I decided to keep my focus on school and work.

On occasion, my job required us to haul off merchandise from the homes of deceased or evicted individuals. Many of the workers began saving items that could be used to make money at the local swap meet. After saving up enough to attend the swap meet, we ended up selling all of our merchandise within three hours and making hundreds of dollars.

I felt just like I had when I was a kid. Everything in my life seemed to be going well. The success I had achieved was remarkable and I was beginning to believe again in my ability to accomplish anything.

It was during this time that I decided the career I wanted to pursue. A friend of mine from CATS had given me a quote from Carl Jung that resonated with me: "If one wishes to understand the human soul, he need not bother with experimental psychology of the laboratory, which can tell him practically nothing. He would be better advised to take off his academic robes, and wander with open heart through the world: through the horrors of prison, insane asylums and hospitals, through dirty, dirty dives and houses of prostitution or gambling, through the drawing rooms of elegant society, the stock exchanges, the socialist meetings, the churches and revival meetings of the cults, to experience love and hate, passion in every form, in his own being...He will come back with wisdom which no five-foot shelf of textbooks could give him and he will be capable of being a doctor to the human soul."

I wanted to pursue a career in social work, and specifically in substance abuse treatment. I had witnessed the devastation that had accompanied my personal substance abuse and the decimation of so many people's minds, bodies, and souls while trapped in addiction. I was extremely passionate about being a part of rebuilding such lives. I wanted to be a part of the fight against social and economic inequalities, I wanted to be engaged in work that was meaningful, and I knew social work could be the catalyst to help me achieve those things. I immediately set the goal of obtaining my associate's degree and intended to follow that with a bachelor's degree in social work.

HEALTH

It was the weekend before my fight and I was stuck in bed with fever-like symptoms. I had been training everyday in preparation for this fight. I was even sparring with professional fighters, some I had fought while they were still amateurs, whenever they came into the boxing gym. I spent the next few days almost completely bedridden, only getting out of bed to train and then back into bed to sleep. I was not sure how I would make it to the fight, but I had been working so hard and I didn't want to pass up this opportunity.

August 19, 2006. Fight day. I was ten pounds lighter than I should have been, my vision was extremely blurry, and I felt absolutely horrible. Friends and acquaintances from my time in CATS had come to watch me fight, so I decided to enter the ring anyway. I wanted to end the fight early, as I was not interested in enduring the full length.

When the bell rang, I came out and knocked the guy down with the first punch. It took me several moments to realize he had been knocked down because my vision was so blurry. I was relieved the fight might be over.

But he stood up. We fought the full length and just as what happened in my last fight, I lost by decision. This came as no surprise to me. My opponent was the brother of the last fighter I had lost to and was related to some of the judges.

Once out of the ring, I continued to feel horrible and ended up in the emergency room that night. After running a full gamut of tests and blood work, the doctor walked into my hospital room with some staggering news. I was diagnosed with diabetes. My current blood sugar level was 920 and the doctor was amazed I was still conscious. Regular blood sugars range between 80 and 120. I should have been in a diabetic coma, so the doctor suggested I remain hospitalized for the next few days.

I thought I would be able to catch up on rest during my hospitalization. I had never stayed at a hospital overnight for medical purposes, but I quickly learned it was not much fun. My blood had to be drawn and tested for sugar levels every two hours. With all of the procedures the hospital staff needed to run, I actually fell further behind on sleep. My new diagnosis required a strict diet than was different than most of the other patients and I felt as I if I was starving. I managed to talk one of the graveyard shift nurses into getting me a sandwich from the cafeteria, as she was unaware of my dietary situation. When the next blood sugar test revealed significantly raised levels, she was severely scolded by her supervisors!

The man I shared a room with was recovering from a heart attack. He must have been about the same age as my father had been when my father was hospitalized for his first heart attack. When his family first visited him, I realized that his family structure was eerily similar to my own: his two children, a girl and a boy, were about four years apart and the daughter was the older of the two. I couldn't help but wonder if this man's children would grow up without a father, as had been my experience. I wondered if this man would make the necessary changes to improve his health upon his release or if he would simply admit defeat and succumb to his physical ailments.

I was released from the hospital after two days and two nights of needles, tests, and blood work. I soon began to realize the significance of diabetes. The diagnosis itself was psychologically challenging. Knowing I had a chronic and progressive disease was disheartening, to say the least. The logistical aspect of managing the disease was equally challenging: testing my sugar throughout the day, evaluating carbohydrate intake, determining the appropriate amount of insulin to take. Needless to say, I struggled to keep my blood sugar in equilibrium.

I immediately went back to work, but I would often take too much insulin and found myself scrambling to get sugar into my system before passing out. Finding the proper balance was a daily struggle. At this time, a fellow employee and I had saved up enough merchandise from work to make another trip to the swap meet. I picked him up early the morning of the swap meet in order to set up our tables and display our goods before people arrived. When I began feeling lightheaded, I made my way to the truck to test my blood sugar. I started shaking so badly that the first test fell out before the machine could read my sugar...

...I awoke with a jolt. I recognized the inside of an ambulance and was laid out on a stretcher, but the sudden awakening had caused me to pull an IV out my arm. The injection of glucose I was given had caused me to wake up. I felt a burning sensation on my head and had a difficult time getting my bearings from the disorientation.

"You've got to lay back down, buddy," the medic instructed me.

"I think I'm going to puke," I managed to mumble. The medics rushed to grab me a garbage can, not wanting vomit in their ambulance, but the nausea passed. I was then bombarded with the standard emergency questions: What's your name? Do you know what day of the week it is? Do you know what year it is?

When I arrived at the hospital, I discovered I had fallen out of the truck and smashed my head on the ground. I had also had a seizure, which dually concerned the doctors given the possible concussion I may have sustained. I was referred to a neurologist upon my release, as well as an endocrinologist and a diabetic educator to assist me with my new life with diabetes. I was still trying to mentally grapple with the long-term implication of my diagnosis; I was not ready to accept living with diabetes.

I went to my sister's house the next weekend for dinner. They had attempted to fix an appropriate meal for me and were asking questions about my newly discovered disease. I knew they were trying to be supportive, but I hated it. I hated being treated like I was disabled, like I needed special attention. I began feeling lightheaded again and asked for some sugar...

...I woke up with police officers, medics, and firemen standing around me in my sister's house. There were stains all over my shirt from the Oreo cookies my sister must have given me. I had experienced another seizure triggered by low blood sugar. My nieces looked extremely worried; I felt completely powerless.

The next few weeks were filled with medical appointments. I was scheduled to first meet with an endocrinologist. Entering her office was like arriving at an oasis in the middle of a desert. Medical facilities were typically so stale and sterile. Her office was full of energy and exuberance, the walls painted different shades of green and accented with flowers. The décor had a very progressive feel to it and I assumed this was that feng shui thing I had heard about!

When I met Dr. Swenson, it was clear to me she was unlike any doctor

I had met before. Her medical expertise aside, she was a true healer. We discussed my personal and family history to help her better understand the context of my diagnosis. To my disgust, she came to the conclusion that my pancreas had likely shut down due to excessive toxins from my years of substance abuse. With all the progress I had made, it felt like I had just taken ten steps backwards, my past coming back to continue wreaking havoc.

After multiple brain scans taken that week, I met with a diabetic educator. She helped me better understand the physiology behind diabetes, the importance of monitoring carbohydrate intake, and the purpose of continual insulin measurements. While the information was incredibly informative, I was somewhat overwhelmed and struggling to accept the lifestyle changes I would need to make.

Next was the neurologist. She had managed to access several brain scans taken in seventh grade and used it to compare my current scans to the scans taken previous to my substance abuse. There were considerable differences. The current scan was full of white spots that had not been present in the original scans. While I didn't fully understand the implications of these spots, several were quite large and disconcerting. We discussed my substance abuse, specifically my methamphetamine use, and she concluded the spots had likely been caused by the excessive substance abuse. The white spots were damaged portions of my brain that no longer functioned properly.

I was staggered. I had been sober for nearly a year at this point, but my body was continuing to fall apart. The damage I had caused to my body was very real and present, whereas the time I had spent causing it seemed like nothing more than a dream.

I continued to train at the boxing center, but it was clear to everyone I was struggling. I was so worried about having low blood sugars that I consistently let them run at high levels. I felt horrible as a result and continued to eat horribly, which only perpetuated the problem. My diabetic educator had run out of ideas. She finally said to me, quite pointedly, "When you are ready to get your health under control, give me a call. There is no reason to continue meeting with me if you aren't ready to make the change yet."

She sounded like a substance abuse counselor! That finding the desire or readiness is necessary for change had often been discussed during my substance abuse treatment. The truth of her words hit home: I wasn't ready to eat healthy and manage my diabetes, and my crazy schedule certainly didn't help with my ability to change my diet.

Even though I was struggling with my health, I was excelling in both school and substance abuse treatment. My grades were good and I was enjoying the stimulation of learning, something I hadn't experienced for over ten years. I continued to face a steep learning curve, particularly the challenges associated with learning how to use current technology. My lack of knowledge surrounding recent world events was a reflection of my "disappearance." I had left the world as most people know it, fallen behind, and was now running at full speed in an attempt to catch up.

RELATIONSHIPS

I completed CATS outpatient treatment in December 2006. Having also successfully completed probation, I needed to attend court both in Sandy City and Taylorsville to have my case closed. When I went to the court in Sandy, my case was immediately closed and I was given kudos from the judge. It felt good to stand in from of the court with the knowledge I had completed treatment and probation successfully; many do not.

I had made a wager with a peer from the CATS program involving a small amount of cash for the one who could get a date first after being released from jail. We had both been out of jail for several months with absolutely no luck in the department of romance! Although my concentration was needed elsewhere, my desire for a connection was still very present. I would soon have a chance to seize the opportunity and secure my winnings.

I found myself waiting to see the judge at the Taylorsville courthouse because of a trial in progress that had exceeded its expected time. Many like me were watching expectantly and waiting to appear before the court. An absolutely gorgeous woman who must have been approximately my age walked into the courtroom out of breath and sat down next to me. "Am I late? Did they start calling names?" she asked with an attractive foreign accent. I explained to her that court had not even started yet, reassuring her she wasn't late. She began complaining about the car problems she was experiencing before asking, "Do you have a car?"

I did not. I had been riding the bus since my release from jail and was afraid this would cause me to miss the opportunity to give her a ride. To my surprise, she asked me if I would like a ride after the proceedings. "I would love a ride," I responded, excited at the prospect of riding with her. My turn finally came. The judge called me to the podium and I presented the requisite documents: a certificate of completion from CATS and a letter of successful completion of probation. My case was closed. I was no longer being monitored by the judicial system and I had a ride home with a beautiful girl with a lovely foreign accent whom I planned to ask on a date. My day was going very well. I informed her I would be waiting for her in the lobby. I immediately called my friend from CATS and left a message on his phone stating he might as well go to the bank and withdraw some money because I was in the process of winning our bet!

When the girl walked into the lobby and we began to leave, she stated she needed to give a friend a ride from work before dropping me off. This was good, as it would give me more time to talk with her and eventually ask her out on a date. We arrived at a Gold's Gym that was still under construction and waited in the parking lot. After a few minutes of chatting, there was a knock at the window. Her "friend" had arrived. It turned out to be her boyfriend! I could not believe it. He even offered to sit in the back seat, but there was no way I was going to sit shotgun with his girlfriend. As we were driving, the man started asking me questions: my name, where I worked, just small talk. Then he asked if I used drugs. I let him know I had been sober for approximately a year. He responded by informing me they both used heroin and I was welcome to have some if I was interested. I thought I was in a nightmare.

"Put your seatbelt on," the man suddenly yelled at his girlfriend. There was a police officer only a few lanes over. She became very agitated and began driving erratically. I could not believe my luck. I had finally resolved all of my legal issues just minutes earlier and here I was in a car with two heroin users swerving all over the road and perhaps seconds away from police contact. She finally managed to maneuver the car into a parking lot where I immediately exited the vehicle and took the bus home. Suffice it to say, I did not win the bet.

I eventually started dating a waitress at a Denny's restaurant. We met while I was doing homework at the diner. She was from a small town and was a year younger than me. We dated frequently and soon became a couple. As our relationship continued to become more serious, she eventually moved in with me. We lived in the basement of my mother's house, similar to our own apartment.

When Jocelyn moved in, I was still attending Salt Lake Community College and decided to enroll in the Alcohol and Drug Abuse Treatment

Training Program (A&D) at the University of Utah. This was a one-year program designed to train students in substance abuse counseling techniques and interventions in preparation for working as licensed professionals in the substance abuse field after graduation. I was working aggressively towards my career goals and preparing to be employed in substance abuse treatment.

One evening during a pharmacology class in the A&D program, a guest speaker came from University of Utah Department of Psychiatry to present to the class. Donna, the clinical director of Assessment and Referral Services (ARS), was looking for student volunteers to facilitate substance abuse support groups for clients waiting to enter treatment. Realizing what an opportunity this would be, I contacted her later that week and was facilitating groups before the end of the month. The work was challenging and being surrounded by professionals with master's and doctoral degrees was intimidating. But I was reminded of the saying, "Surround yourself with successful people," and I knew this could only be in my best interest.

Jocelyn and I had begun tentatively planning a date to get married, but our plans changed significantly when we made the decision to conceive a child. It seemed that we could not wait to start our life together and felt ready to take this meaningful step in our relationship. This sped up our marriage plans, as we decided to have the wedding while Jocelyn could still fit in a wedding dress! We were married in December 2007, in a small chapel. Our honeymoon took place at a beautiful three-story historic bed and breakfast in Salt Lake City.

I recognized I was developing a meaningful life, which was completely in opposition to what I had known for so long. I felt like my life was finally going in a positive direction, that Jocelyn and I were on our way to true happiness.

The A&D program required a three hundred hour internship during the second semester. As I interviewed with various agencies, I encountered a string of denials based on my criminal background. This was extremely frustrating. I felt like all the progress I had made was for nothing. When Donna, my supervisor at ARS, referred me to First Step House, I was accepted as an intern and began case managing clients. This was the same agency I was originally supposed to attend treatment before I enrolled in CATS. It turned out I would be spending some time there after all, not as a client, but as an intern. As the world turns.

The weekend after beginning at First Step House, my mother and I were shopping at Target when I began feeling shaky. I ran immediately to the car to get my blood sugar monitor. When I reentered the store, my vision was foggy and I was becoming increasingly disoriented. I eventually found my mother and began testing my sugar.

I woke up surrounded by at least twenty people: interested customers, store employees, firemen, and medics. One of the medics began shoving a disgusting gel into my mouth and I nearly vomited. Apparently I had another seizure due to my low blood sugar. The embarrassment and helplessness I felt were surreal. These incidents were beginning to be very trying on my psyche. I felt like I had no control, that my body was failing me. The only explanation I had was a toxic past that was continuing to haunt all aspects of my life.

My wife and I attended appointment after appointment with various doctors in an effort to get my diabetes under control. But just like my blood sugar, our relationship was suffering from many ups and downs. We were struggling to communicate effectively and at one point were hardly speaking to each other at all. We began attending couples counseling in an attempt to salvage our relationship, but it was simply not enough. Jocelyn decided to return to her hometown and I filed for divorce. She was approximately five months pregnant at this point. I was becoming more and more concerned about my ability to be present in my child's life.

I completed my internship at First Step House almost immediately after Jocelyn left, but I decided to continue there as a volunteer. Not only did I want to stay connected with the agency, but also I was having trouble with divorce, feeling empty and lost, and staying busy seemed to help me cope. I was hired on by ARS as a part-time employee and I began running as many groups a week as my schedule would allow.

I saw many familiar faces while running groups at ARS, people I knew from CATS who hadn't remained sober, people I had met on the streets, and people I had been incarcerated with. I heard particularly troubling news from one guy: Linda's daughter, Kristi, had died of an Oxycontin overdose and Jesse Cochran, my cellmate and acquaintance from the streets, had been shot and killed by the police in an attempt to escape arrest.

With everything that was going on in my life, this was hard news to hear. I felt like we were all dying, Kristi, Jesse, myself. I had simply been sentenced to a slow and arduous death through diabetes and epilepsy. When I looked up the police incident with Jesse on the Internet, I learned he had nearly run over an officer when he was fired upon. I couldn't help but think of the negative impact his death would have on so many lives. Jesse was only twenty-five years old. His child would grow up without a father; his family would mourn and try to understand where they had gone wrong. And even though the police officer had done the right thing, he would likely be affected for the rest of his life, playing the scene over in his mind and wondering if there was another way the situation could have turned out: an unnecessary death averted and Jesse still living.

NEW LIFE

July 8, 2008. Ashlyn Beverly Bryant was born. I received a call early in the morning informing me that Jocelyn had gone into labor. My mother and I began the two-hour car ride to the small rural town in eastern Utah. I received a message en route: Ashlyn had already been born. I was furious that I didn't get to experience her birth, but stunned at the realization that a new life had been brought into the world.

When we finally arrived, I realized I had never seen a newborn baby before. As I held Ashlyn in my arms, I couldn't help but think about how tiny and fragile she was. She was absolutely beautiful. I traveled back to Salt Lake City later that day. I was troubled about how very little influence I would have on my daughter's upbringing, but even more concerned about her being raised in such a negative atmosphere. A few weeks later, I received a call in the middle of the night informing me Jocelyn had been in a car accident. The Department of Child and Family Services (DCFS) had taken custody of Ashlyn when Jocelyn tested positive for methamphetamine. Without notifying me, DCFS took Ashlyn to a foster family while I frantically attempted to get in touch with them in an effort to get my daughter.

I received temporary custody of Ashlyn a few days later in court. Jocelyn was granted the opportunity for reunification upon submission of random drug tests and completion of a substance abuse treatment program. I was deeply concerned about the possibility of losing custody of my daughter, but realized Jocelyn was so entrenched in her addiction that she was not likely to comply with the court's orders.

I graduated a week later from the Alcohol and Drug Abuse Treatment Training Program at the University of Utah. It was an incredible feeling to have completed something meaningful. I also received my Associate of Science degree from Salt Lake Community College that same week. First Step House decided to hire me as a full-time employee, case managing clients and facilitating substance abuse treatment groups. I was well on my way to successfully achieving my goals and establishing a career in substance abuse treatment.

The past year had certainly been eventful. I had conceived a child, gotten married, been hired at Assessment and Referral Services, experienced marital strife and subsequent divorce, witnessed the birth of my daughter, gained custody of my daughter, completed an associate's degree and the A&D program, and been hired full-time at First Step House. Whew! It was a very challenging year in sobriety. Despite all of these challenges, relapse never even entered into my consciousness, but I was beginning to believe than living a responsible life was much more difficult and painful than the addiction of my past.

Jocelyn's lack of compliance with any of the stipulations outlined by DCFS resulted in an additional court hearing to determine custody. Jocelyn didn't even show up. It was a clear reflection of the influence of addiction on priorities. I was given full permanent custody of Ashlyn with visitation from Jocelyn at my discretion. I was relieved.

On my way out of the courthouse, I saw Crystal, the lady from the house on the north side who had a child with the now deceased Jesse. She was also receiving custody of her child that day due to her completion of Drug Court, a treatment program run by the courts. It was only a few weeks later I saw Crystal walking down State Street without her child, strung out on drugs. Another family ruined by addiction.

AS THE WORLD TURNS

Working at First Step House was very fulfilling; leading treatment groups and working with clients was incredibly rewarding. I felt like I was making a difference in people's lives. When one of my very first clients came to the agency for his initial appointment, an eerily familiar tattoo read 33LLC, the acronym for the Thirty-Third Lay Low Crip gang. This was the gang Rob belonged to, the man I was with when I was first arrested. It was also the gang of the trustee who traded commissary for tobacco when I was incarcerated.

Despite my preconceived notions, this client was one of my most successful and eventually completed treatment. He brought his brother along for his graduation: the trustee I had known from jail. He was now in a wheelchair, the victim of a shooting. The number of lives affected by drugs and crime was becoming increasingly evident to me while working as a substance abuse counselor.

But this client was a success. Witnessing recovery can be a truly beautiful thing. It helped create hope for me and continues to do so, hope that drug addiction can be overcome and hope that one day the problem will be better addressed in society. While incarcerated, I heard an analogy involving a clam that I feel gives justice to the process of recovery. When the clam gets a grain of sand in its shell that it cannot get rid of, the sand irritates the clam's tender skin and becomes extremely painful. The clam reacts to this irritant by covering the grain of sand with layer after layer of skin. The result, after much pain and irritation, is a beautiful and highly prized pearl, similar to a recovered addict.

Reflecting on my personal recovery progress has made me recognize its significance, the significant changes I had made in my life. It made me feel good. I finally felt like I was beginning to fulfill my potential by accomplishing both personal and professional goals. This became especially evident to me while attending my ARS holiday party in 2008. I was talking with my supervisor, Donna, when a lady with bright red hair walked into the room. I did a double take. "Is that lady's name Jill?" I asked Donna. "Yes. Do you know her?" she responded. This redheaded lady was the same individual who had performed my assessment in jail. I couldn't believe it. I explained to my supervisor how I recognized her. Donna tried to convince me to go and talk to her, but I didn't want to. Seeing her was more than enough. Not only was I working for First Step House, the agency I had originally been referred to, but I was also working for ARS, the agency responsible for my assessment in jail. The synchronicities were almost eerie. It seemed as if my life had truly come full circle.

FRUSTRATION

After completing the A&D program, I needed to obtain a license to work as a substance abuse counselor. I submitted my application to the Department of Professional Licensing (DOPL) anticipating I would be required to meet with the licensing board due to my criminal background. When I arrived at the meeting, I discovered that the executive directors from both ARS and First Step House, as well as one of my teachers from the program, were on the board.

The meeting began with a discussion concerning my criminal background. One by one, every criminal charge on my record was divulged, discussed, and dissected. I wanted to crawl into a hole. I was so ashamed. All of the board members were highly respected individuals in the substance abuse field and I hated being placed under the microscope by them. The meeting resulted in a temporary denial of my license pending further information.

I was devastated. I felt stuck in a void. While I had managed to completely detach myself from the world of drugs and crime, my past still haunted me. I was stuck in limbo, not yet accepted into the tribe of substance abuse professionals.

It was at this time I began my coursework at the University of Utah in the Bachelor of Social Work program. I was determined not to let the setback with DOPL hinder my progress; I knew continuing my education would only increase my ability to be successful. My enrollment in the program was a very wise decision. I not only thoroughly enjoyed the coursework, but I was also increasing my capacity to assist others in improving their lives. I was doing everything in my power to grow professionally.

MAN'S BEST FRIEND

My dog, Oscar, a boxer like my other dog, was truly a kindred soul. His birthday was the day before mine, he was born with a congenital heart disease like me, and we both had heart murmurs that had potential for further complications. He was a friend that had been there to comfort me through some of the worst times in my life. Oscar was getting older, experiencing joint problems, and slowing down. Even with all of his discomfort, he was still extremely patient with my daughter. She would poke and prod at him, grab his tail for fun, and he would simply look at me with his dog smile.

One morning, my mother hastily woke me up and frantically tried explaining that I needed to get out of bed, that Oscar wasn't doing well. I jumped out of bed to find him lying in a pool of blood and struggling to breathe. We rushed him to the hospital where he was placed on oxygen, but his breathing grew more and more labored. The veterinarian walked in, like a scene in a movie, fumbling over the words to explain Oscar's critical situation. There was nothing that could be done for him; he would have to be put to sleep. I could hardly talk or think; my emotions had taken control of my ability to function. Oscar had been my best friend.

The doctor hesitantly explained that he needed our permission to put Oscar to sleep. We were asked how we would pay for the procedure and informed we would need to do so prior to its implementation. My mind lurched back in time: when my father died, we were not allowed to mourn, we had to pick a casket, we had to find a burial plot, we had to transport his body from Albuquerque, we had to plan his services, it was all very expensive…

I was outraged. What if we were unable to procure the money? What would happen then? Would Oscar have to die slowly and painfully? Would we have to watch him suffer and struggle to breathe? So we paid. We were led into the room where Oscar was lying on the examination table. He was ecstatic to see us and attempted to lift his head off the table to greet us. There was so much life left in his eyes, but his body was no longer capable of holding his spirit. The vet administered the lethal dose of drugs and as the life faded from Oscar's eyes, I simultaneously collapsed.

I floated in and out of consciousness, waking to people trying to give me sugar and others asking me questions. The ambulance finally arrived to check my sugar; it was low, but not critical. Oscar's spirit had left this plane of existence.

SUCCESS

When I attended my substance abuse license review, my supervisor at ARS, Donna, joined me in order to speak on my behalf. I was incredibly nervous; if I did not obtain licensure today, it was likely I would never be eligible. With the board, we reviewed some of the additional information that had been provided and then Donna was given the chance to speak on my behalf. This appeared to make all the difference, as I was granted a probationary license. I found myself continuing to reap the rewards of recovery.

I had observed many people using Alcoholics Anonymous (AA) as a social support group to be more successful in recovery. I had begun attending these meetings as a requirement of CATS outpatient treatment, but continued to attend frequently after graduating from CATS. AA celebrates sobriety birthdays, landmarks of sobriety, by passing out coins to mark the attained period of abstinence. September 26, 2009 was the day I received my four-year coin.

This year had been especially meaningful to me: I had come so far in school, work, my personal life, and all while being sober in the short span of four years. I had also just applied to a master of social work program. This marked a fulfillment of a momentous period of progress for me. Four years previous I was being arrested for breaking into a condemned house wearing the same clothes for an entire week with a backpack full of stolen fruit pies. My old life was like a bad dream—my progress felt great.

I also recognized the great deal of hardship I had experienced in recovery. The divorce coupled with receiving custody of my daughter had been emotionally trying. My health issues rendered day-to-day life much more challenging. I was discovering that life in sobriety was much harder than simply getting high all day because I was beginning to care. I cared about other people's well being as well as my own. I cared about achieving success, a multitude of additional responsibilities in itself. I was learning to care about life. I found that this felt good. This helped me foster hope.

CLOSE CALL

Having just finished a three-mile run and a boxing workout, I felt great. I showered and headed to work at First Step House. As the afternoon wore on, I started feeling ill and soon became nauseous. After multiple trips to the bathroom to vomit, I was still feeling under the weather. I soon left, went to my other job at ARS, and arrived early while continuing to feel flu-like symptoms. My blood sugar continued to drop because I couldn't keep any food down. As other employees arrived, I had to excuse myself from work.

I initially thought to stop at a local health clinic to have some sugar injected, but decided to tough it out until I got home for financial reasons. It took only a couple of minutes for me to realize I would not be able to make it home. Rather than call for an ambulance myself, I called my mother and asked her to call an ambulance. My thoughts were foggy and disconnected. I told her to have them meet me at the Denny's directly off of the freeway exit. Ironically, this was the same Denny's where I had met my ex-wife. How interesting. I just needed to make it to the Denny's, just had to keep driving and make it to Denny's...

...I awoke with a jolt before recognizing I was still in my car driving through gravel on the side of the freeway. But I was headed directly for a metal sign. I swerved momentarily back onto the freeway, narrowly missing the sign, before pulling over to the side of the road. My attempts to get to Denny's had almost proved as disastrous as my marriage. My body's emergency response system was the only thing that had saved me, but the bile that rose to my throat was indication enough that I was not yet in the clear.

A car had witnessed my erratic driving and pulled over to assist me. A female passenger stepped out and asked if I needed any help. As I continued to vomit, I told her I needed an ambulance. Utah Highway Patrol arrived first and the officer attempted talking to me to keep me comfortable and calm. It was clear that he was the one in need of comfort; my diabetes and continual vomiting were way out of his league and he looked incredibly worried!

I eventually made it to the hospital, but nearly passed out on the gurney. When I was finally given a glucose injection, my body went into shock. I began shaking violently, my teeth were chattering, and I felt bitter cold. This continued for over an hour and I was physically exhausted by the time the whole ordeal was over. Every muscle in my body was sore from the shaking and I was completely sapped of energy.

Although I have had a few close calls in regards to my health, this one really opened my eyes. I have a daughter who depends on me and a life I've worked hard to create. I realized how fragile life is, both hers and mine. My journey through addiction and recovery and transition to a meaningful life is not over. I have much more to accomplish, but I am confident I will continue to persevere.

Writing this book has been exhausting, mentally and emotionally, but also exalting, sometimes painful, but also enlightening. I have encountered more people from my past during my writing than ever before. Ranging from the first person to sell me drugs to childhood friends entering treatment in an effort to improve their lives and live free of addiction, these encounters have spanned the spectrum from surreal to serendipitous. These synchronicities have made this literary journey both emotionally difficult and personally fulfilling.

It's interesting being on the other side of addiction, on the flip side of the proverbial coin. I spent years entrenched in my drug addiction, nearly a decade ensnared in the haze of intoxication, victim to the whims of the monster that seemingly inhabited my body. Substance abuse is not foreign to me. Addiction is not a stranger. It is an intimate shadow that continues to permeate my life, professionally, personally, sometimes exonerating, often plaguing. I witness transformations in addict's lives as I continue to work for the agency I was initially referred to for treatment, as well as the agency that assessed me. I observe the struggling, the dedication, and the anguish required to overcome addiction.

But I also see the pain, the failure, and the loss. My ex-wife has been released from jail, but I'm angry and fearful. I find myself defensive, pending the outcome. Will she continue to use? Will she make an effort to turn her life around? When is she going to mess up? It's sort of ironic being on the opposite end, recognizing the feelings that others must have felt towards me for all those years. Angry at what has transpired due to addiction, fearful of the future, struggling for hope. But this is where I am now. Struggling for hope. Looking to the future. Curious to see how my life will unfold. *As the world turns...*